THE COMPANION PLANTING PLAYBOOK FOR BEGINNERS

A SIMPLE 7-STEP GUIDE TO THRIVING GARDENS, NATURAL PEST CONTROL, AND BOUNTIFUL CROPS

P. JOSEPH RICHARDS

CONTENTS

INTRODUCTION

There's this running joke amongst home gardeners that the plants in your garden die if you look at them funny. Meanwhile, dandelions grow out of the cracks in a sidewalk. I'm pretty sure I speak for everyone when I say we've all committed accidental mass "floracide" before (get it? "flora" as in plant life and "homicide" as in... Never mind.)

But what if I told you that it's possible to turn your garden space into a self-sustaining ecosystem, no matter how much space you have to work with? Oh yes! Imagine having a garden that—with a little bit of initial effort—is easier to maintain and keep alive in the long term. It sounds too good to be true, except it isn't. Companion planting builds on the foundation of permaculture gardening. And it's revolutionary.

There is such an overwhelming amount of information on gardening that it's no wonder many beginner gardeners put off getting started. You can only get started if you know where to begin in the first place.

By implementing the permaculture gardening technique of companion planting, you can manage and prevent all major gardening qualms, such as poor soil quality, ineffective pest control, weed management, and underperforming crops. Another thing many novice gardeners worry about is space. In today's economy, you're lucky to have a balcony, not to mention a small backyard.

While you need space to grow a garden, I've seen people grow enough strawberry plants in PVC pipes mounted against a wooden fence to feed a small army. Even in that aspect, permaculture has got you covered! And yes, you also need quality soil for a thriving garden, so even if you inherited a chunk of land from your grandma, it will only help if the soil's good. But once again, there's a way to fix it.

You may have grown a few tomatoes ages ago, but the aphids were so rampant they destroyed the whole yield before you could taste your hard work. I get it. It's exceptionally demotivating to put in months (sometimes even years) of hard work to have it disappear almost overnight. This problem is really where companion planting thrives: natural and organic pest control, resilience, and self-sufficiency.

Another common reason why many people are discouraged from taking the leap and starting (or expanding) their home gardens is time. You and every other adult in your household likely have a full-time job on top of other personal and familial responsibilities. You barely have time to juggle everything else, let alone a needy garden. But that's just the thing: when you leave nature up to nature (as is the case with companion planting), most of the gardening work that's usually considered laborious and time-consuming is taken care of *for* you.

With companion planting, you drastically minimize your time in your garden while reaping bountiful harvests. In addition, you significantly reduce your need for fertilizer or harmful pesticides or herbicides. You'll be saving money, time, and space.

The seven steps to companion planting outlined throughout this book focus on the "GROWER" method. It's an acronym that encompasses and includes all the necessary information you need to know, all condensed into one source. The acronym stands for:

- **G**et to know companion planting (chapter 1).

Regardless of your situation, you'll discover what it is and why it's the best option.

- **R**esearch the science (chapter 2).

We'll discuss why companion planting works so well by exploring science-based evidence.

- **O**ptimize the benefits (chapter 3).

You'll learn how to plan your garden to maximize all the fantastic benefits of companion planting.

- **W**ise pairings (chapters 4-7).

Discover an in-depth guide to tested and proven guilds and companions for vegetables, fruits, herbs, and flowers.

- Environment-specific strategies (chapters 8-10).

How to maximize planting in limited spaces, improve soil health, manage pests, and consider different climates.

- Resolve and refine (chapter 11).

Discover things to keep in mind, troubleshooting, and additional tips and tricks for companion planting.

If you've read any of my other books, you know that I grew up on a farm where my parents implemented some permaculture approaches. I was exposed to it growing up but only really put a little thought into it. We had a compost pile, mulched our crops, and saved rainwater, but nothing major. But as I grew up, I started seeing the benefits and impact of what a little bit could do, so I had to know more. Permaculture has leveled up my gardening skills. Our farm requires less work than ever, and our harvests are abundant.

Whether you want to turn a piece of land into a food forest or enjoy a few fresh herbs for everyday use, companion planting will ensure you get there with less effort and time spent in the grand scheme of things.

So many aspiring gardeners give up on trying after failing so many times or think that because they don't have a patch of grass, all hope is out the window. I'm here to tell you that if gardening is your passion (that you're not planning on giving up on any time soon), this is the only guide you need to bring your vision of a low-maintenance garden to life—no matter your circumstances.

You won't just be growing a garden but cultivating a healthier, more sustainable, and uniquely fulfilling lifestyle.

1

COMPANION PLANTING BASICS

P lants "talk" to each other. That sounds like some new-aged, sci-fi mumbo-jumbo, but it's true. Of course, it's not a language you and I can understand or even hear; instead, they mainly communicate chemically and via underground mycorrhizal (a type of fungi) networks. Through this type of communication, plants often alter their behavior or even share nutrients and resources in response to environmental changes or cues.

However, a recent study found that plants also emit ultrasonic "clicking" sounds that might be audible to insects and certain mammals (Khait et al., 2023). It still needs to be determined whether these sounds are intentional (used for communication, to attract pollinators, or to distract predators) or are just a result of microscopic, physiological processes within the plant itself.

Researchers can say that the frequency of the clicking sounds sounded different when a plant was healthy versus when it was distressed (dehydrated or cut). Remember that this doesn't necessarily prove that the sounds are because of pain or distress; it's simply a response. Either way, this discovery is both profoundly fascinating and unsettling at the same time.

However, there are several reasons why some plants might not "get along" with certain other plants. Welcome to your garden's social media network!

WHAT IS COMPANION PLANTING?

When you think of a garden, you envision traditional monocultural farming practices. Everything you plant is separated; there's an allocated spot or garden bed for your beans, far away from your tomatoes, and so on. However, monocultures are destructive for many reasons: they strip the soil, damage biodiversity, lead to pest infestations, and result in having to use large amounts of chemical fertilizers and pesticides for a satisfactory harvest.

Companion planting is an alternative approach to monocultures. It involves planting different crops close to each other so they benefit each other by providing ground cover, weed management, natural pest control, and so much more. But companion planting also helps the soil, attracts pollinators, saves space, and increases yields and better-quality produce.

This gardening method falls under permaculture practices and has been practiced worldwide for thousands of years. We are still determining exactly when companion planting started, most likely because it dates back to the nomadic hunter-gatherer era, where barely anything was well-documented.

The "three sisters" method, discovered by Native Americans, is a notable example of companion planting still in use today. The "three sisters" refers to planting beans, corn, and squash together in a guild. The corn is stable support for the climbing beans; the beans replace the nitrogen in the soil (keeping it fertile), and the squash covers the ground, preventing the soil from drying out (the leaves are also used as mulch once the season is over).

Companion planting forms a network of protection and mutual benefit for every plant. Every plant has a function and contributes to a self-sustaining ecosystem in your backyard (even if that function only provides you with food). By observing nature and working with it, you make your own life more manageable.

Does It Work?

Many skeptics say no scientific evidence supports the idea that companion planting is better than the average gardener or farmer's practices. Putting aside the fact that it makes your garden subjectively easier to maintain, there *is* solid, irrefutable proof that companion planting is highly beneficial on more than one front:

- Companion planting improves soil quality (Zhang et al., 2018) (Chen et al., 2020) (Xiao et al., 2013).
- Companion planting inhibits harmful bacteria growth that can affect the health of your plants and their root systems (van Elsas et al., 2012) (Xu et al., 2014) (Fu et al., 2016).
- Companion planting is effective for pest resistance (Riesselman, n.d.) (Saldanha et al., 2019) (Ben-Issa et al., 2017).
- Companion planting improves yield size and produce quality (Griffiths-Lee et al., 2020) (Montoya et al., 2020).

Whether you believe it works or not, companion planting is a natural observation. Nature always finds the easiest, most efficient way to do things because it has had tens of millions of years to figure it out. To go against that is to create endless work and, more often than not, perpetual disappointment for yourself.

Why It Works

Imagine you want to start a town from scratch for a second. What does a city need for it to thrive and be productive? Besides the physical infrastructure (buildings, roads, etc.), police officers, teachers, doctors, firefighters, builders, plumbers, electricians, business owners, cashiers, cleaners, sanitation workers, etc.

A garden is like a plant version of a town, with many essential roles to fill. Can a city occupied solely by police officers, for example, be productive? It would probably be the safest town, but what happens when a fire breaks out, a sewage pipe clogs, or a flu outbreak?

That's precisely the issue with monocultural agriculture. As much as we need to create a multifaceted community to fulfill everyone's needs, we need to foster diversity in every aspect. All the plants have separate functions and goals with companion planting, but they ultimately work together as a unit. Some plants strip the soil to provide food, while the plants beside it ward off pests and replenish the soil.

Certain types of crops will benefit your garden in different ways, but here are some things you stand to gain regardless of the types of plants you decide to grow in your garden:

- Maintaining Soil Health.

Crop plants always extract water, minerals, and nutrients from the soil to grow and reproduce through seeds. As you likely know, nitrogen, phosphorus, and potassium are the three most essential nutrients for the soil to stay fertile and support plant growth.

Companion planting will reduce your need to continuously fertilize your garden because some plants (like legumes and clover) are "nitrogen-fixers," meaning they put the nitrogen from the air back into the soil. Root vegetables prevent soil from becoming compacted. The remaining plant matter is left in the ground at the end of the season or used as mulch to replace phosphorus. The diversity that companion planting offers also helps maintain and establish helpful microorganism populations that live in the soil beneath your garden (which also contributes to healthy roots and plants).

- Pest Control.

Certain plants have natural pest-deterring capabilities, whether it be through emitting strong smells that ward off pests in general or camouflaging attractive smells (from fruits or vegetables), releasing certain chemicals into the ground or air, or simply attracting predatory insects that feed on harmful ones.

- Weed Management.

That's right! You can minimize or even prevent weeds from growing in your garden. There are two ways this can happen. The first is that some plants release chemicals that slow the growth of weeds, effectively keeping them in check. The second is planting ground cover crops in all the bare spaces in your garden (like clover, alfalfa, or creeping thyme) to suppress weeds from taking over in the first place.

- Maximizing Space.

Companion planting lets you plan your garden bed to fit more plants in a smaller space. By considering the different growth rates and root systems of the different types of plants, you can maximize your available garden space. You can plant a crop with a shallow root system way closer to a crop that has a taproot system because they won't compete for space underground.

The key is to be strategic about your crop placements and timing. Radishes, for example, grow so fast that they'll need to be harvested way before your carrots need that extra space. So, even though carrots and radishes are both root vegetables, you can plant your radishes in between your carrots with no issues!

- Increased Yields.

This result is more due to a combination of all the other benefits of companion planting. Fewer pests mean less loss of plant foliage and fruit, more biodiversity means more pollinators and better soil quality means healthier plants (and therefore more and better-quality produce).

PERMACULTURE PRINCIPLES

You don't need to adopt or implement permaculture principles in every aspect of your gardening regime; however, companion planting focuses on these principles. It would only be fitting to explore these principles briefly.

Permaculture is a portmanteau of "permanent" and "agriculture." The essence of this practice is to design any garden or farm space based on systems that are naturally present to work with Mother Nature rather than against it. Sustainability (for you and your garden) and self-sufficiency are at the core of permaculture practices.

Garden Ecosystems

Companion planting is integral to permaculture because it creates a self-sufficient, resilient, thriving garden. And again, even if you don't commit to all permaculture gardening principles, implementing companion planting involves creating an entire interconnected ecosystem in your backyard.

A garden ecosystem includes the following:

- Biodiversity.

All living organisms, including plants, insects, pests, fungi, and bacteria, contribute to the health of your garden. A diverse garden will attract life in all forms; that's a given. The aim is to create a natural balance between predator and prey—a circle of life. Your tomato plants attract aphids, ladybugs eat the aphids, and ladybugs attract birds, frogs, spiders, and dragonflies to your garden, which is good for pollination and keeping other types of pests under control.

Despite how you feel about spiders or other creepy crawlies, having them visit your garden is good. This biodiversity contributes to natural pest control, pollination, decomposition, increased yields, and a happy garden.

- Soil Microbiology.

At the beginning of this chapter, we talked about how plants communicate with each other through underground fungal networks. But there's more going on in the ground underneath your cabbage patch. Fungi, bacteria, and even worms all play an essential role in nutrient cycling and soil formation.

Many permaculture gardeners have worm farms and collect worm castings and something called "worm tea" (the liquid that seeps out of the worm farm, and yes, it's as disgusting as it sounds) to use as fertilizer in their garden beds. That's how valuable these slimy little creatures are!

The same principles that count above ground also apply to the underground population. You want to maintain a balance where the beneficial bacteria and microorganisms are thriving so the harmful ones don't take over and lead to the death of your garden.

That is why biodiversity in your garden is so crucial. A healthy and diverse ecosystem will keep your garden thriving indefinitely without you having to drench the Earth in chemicals or give up more of your valuable time trying to fight nature (to no avail).

CONCERNS ABOUT COMPANION PLANTING

Whether you're still on the fence or all in, I'm sure you have some concerns. It will require a lot of additional research (even after you read this book) and even some trial and error to achieve your gardening goals. Companion planting will help you get there regardless of your ambitions.

We will now be addressing the most common concerns relating to companion planting to set your mind at ease:

- Time Investment.

With an already busy schedule, the last thing you want to hear is that it will take longer. And the honest answer is that companion planting will require you to invest more time initially. The research, planning, and preparation will be the most challenging and time-consuming.

So yes, initially, it will be more time-consuming. However, in the long run, it will pay off. Imagine a garden with little to no weeds, minimum need for fertilization, no significant pest problems, and no need for chemical treatments. Now imagine, on top of that, the best yield your garden can manage to offer. That initial time investment will lead to your only general garden maintenance: stroll through it once a week to ensure everything is running smoothly and harvesting once the time comes.

- Space Requirements.

Again, while gardening requires some outdoor space (or at least a sunny windowsill or balcony), only gardening techniques like companion planting will maximize the available space. We will discuss this topic in more detail later, but you can grow more food in a smaller space than you think is possible.

Besides the fact that companion planting utilizes every inch of available space you have, other methods further help this, like vertical gardens, container planting, or making a raised garden bed on top of solid concrete. With a little bit of strategic planning, you can go far.

- Effectiveness.

The big question: Is it worth it? It depends on your gardening goals; I need help answering this question. When you look at the benefits of companion planting and the evidence that backs it up objectively, the answer is yes. You need to evaluate your goals and what you want your garden to be and decide whether companion planting will aid your approach or strategy to achieve the desired results. The answer is usually yes.

Now that you know the basics of companion planting and what to expect going forward, deciding whether you want to turn the page is up to you. Please put on your lab coat because next, we'll dive into the science of companion planting and why certain plants work so well together. Don't worry, it's pretty interesting.

2

THE SCIENCE BEHIND COMPANION PLANTING

I t's not magic; it's just science. Certain plants are helpful to certain other species of plants and vice versa, helping each other thrive by keeping the soil healthy, fending off pests, protecting each other from diseases or other environmental factors, or, in some cases, contributing to taste. But usually, it's a combination of all the above mentioned.

In this chapter, you'll learn about plant chemistry and the communication happening in the soil. And as dull as that may sound, it will answer most (if not all) of your questions about companion planting. You'll understand why it's an effective pest management strategy and how it contributes to soil health. We'll also be debunking some common myths about companion planting.

UNDERSTANDING PLANT CHEMISTRY

Just like our brains release endorphins and other chemical messages that keep us alive and determine how we react to our environment, plants have a similar process called allelopathy. Allelopathy is how a plant grows and defends itself from diseases or pests. But these chemicals also affect the health of the soil and all living organisms surrounding it (other plants, weeds, microorganisms, and insects). It also affects how plants talk and respond to each other.

The effects of these allelochemicals can be either directly or indirectly beneficial or harmful. Allelopathy is how a plant recognizes it's in danger. Based on the kind of danger (pests, pathogens, or competition in the form of overcrowding or weeds), it will release certain chemicals into the soil or even into the air that can inhibit the growth of competitor plants and weeds, ward off pests, and kill pathogens (bacteria, viruses, fungi, etc.) Allelopathy is so effective that researchers use it to create more effective organic pesticides.

These chemicals are known as volatile organic compounds (or VOCs) and include substances from a plant's secondary metabolic or decomposition systems, for example, water-soluble organic acids, straight-chain alcohols, ketones, amino acids, phenols, and long-chain fatty acids to name but a few.

When I first heard the phrase VOCs, my brain immediately thought of the word "biohazard." The word "volatile" is both accurate and not accurate when referring to plant chemistry. Volatility in plants is an entirely natural process; snake poison and cyanide, considered biohazards, are both naturally occurring compound chemicals. But I digress.

While VOCs are crucial to survival, producing allelochemicals can lead to autotoxicity (when a plant accidentally kills itself) and soil sickness (the chemicals released by the plant make the soil uninhabitable). Managing plant allelopathy is crucial for crop growth. Crop rotation, intercropping, and companion planting can help. When plants are happy and not fighting over resources, they work together.

Specific compounds are released depending on the threat or situation at hand. So, the type of VOC released when there's a drought is different from when there's a bacterial disease present in the soil, and so on. But VOCs are also responsible for attracting pollinators and other beneficial organisms and repelling certain pests. These chemical reactions within the roots are also how plants "communicate" with microorganisms in the soil and form a mutually beneficial relationship.

For example, plant roots release sugars and other organic acids (including nitrogen) into the soil. Then microorganisms (bacteria and mycorrhizae) will "eat" and break these compounds down, making them more accessible (or usable) to the plant. Soil microorganisms also form a protection barrier around the plant's roots, making the environment hostile to pathogens that seek to harm the plant.

THE MECHANISMS BEHIND NATURAL PEST CONTROL

Arguably, the most sought-after benefit of companion planting is the element of natural pest control. You're not spraying harmful chemicals on your plants that can seep into the soil. You're letting nature take its course by creating an environment where pest populations are kept in line (not eradicated, but managed); you're encouraging a circle of life and using it to your advantage. In addition, you can use structural strategies to control and minimize pest populations further.

Ideally, you want to integrate natural pest management protocols into your garden when designing it according to permaculture principles. However, there is always time to introduce natural pest management, regardless of where you may be in your gardening journey.

We'll cover the most common and effective mechanisms and techniques behind integrated pest management. Depending on the type and severity of the pests in your garden, you'll have to decide which method (or combination of them) will work best for your specific situation. You may have to tailor your approach to get the best results. Nevertheless, here are the most common ways to naturally manage pests:

- Predator Attraction.

Inviting predatory insects to your garden helps control the pest populations in a few ways. Certain adult insects themselves will feast on the pests, or their larvae will. You can encourage predatory insects to stick around by providing for their basic needs: food, water, and shelter.

Pollen and nectar from your crops (and even the presence of pests) provide them with food. Lots of foliage shelters them (you can also build insect homes by drilling holes in blocks of untreated wood and placing them around your garden). Dew droplets on leaves provide them with water, but you can take it a step further by putting out water in shallow bowls filled with pebbles (the pebbles prevent small insects from accidentally drowning and give them something to crawl onto if they do fall in the water).

- Pest Repellent Crops.

Some crops (typically herbs) are strong-scented and will deter certain types of pests because they don't like the smell. A few common examples of pest-repellent aromatic herbs are mint, garlic, coriander, chives, and thyme.

Plant aromatic, pest-repellent herbs and flowers along the perimeter or edges of your garden and between your crops (interplanting).

- Trap Cropping.

Trap cropping involves sacrificing one or two plants to lure pests away from the rest of your garden. Different pests prefer different crops; slugs favor lettuce, budworms, and aphids go after tomatoes, beetles and weevils feed mainly on legume leaves, and so on. However, they will make do with whatever your garden has to offer if need be.

The idea is to provide the pests in your garden with an all-you-can-eat buffet of their favorite fruit or vegetable. This tactic will prevent them from infiltrating your entire yield. So, if you find slugs on your tomatoes, for example, grow a single lettuce plant nearby. The slugs will choose the lettuce over the tomatoes any day of the week. Yes, you will likely destroy the lettuce plant, and you won't be able to harvest from it, but your tomatoes will remain untouched.

Furthermore, you can inspect your sacrificial crops now and then and manually remove any pests or eggs you come across. Remove the entire plant and replace it with another to eliminate tiny pests like aphids that have overrun the trap crop. Removing pests isn't ideal, but it can help keep the population from growing out of control.

In some cases, planting trap crops around the border or edge of your garden bed works well; other times, you might have to interplant the trap crops. However, this will depend on the type of pest, their population, and determination.

- Create Confusion.

Interplanting strong-scented herbs and rotating your crops can contribute to confusion. Aromas from herbs carry through the wind and can mask the smell of your fruits and vegetables to a degree. This confusion means pests will be less likely to stumble across your garden or follow the sweet smell of dinner. Moreover, rotating your crops adds to the confusion and positively affects soil health (two birds, one stone).

- Structural Strategies.

If nothing works to minimize or prevent pest infestations, turn to physical barriers. You can do this through mesh-covered frames or tunnels (over a plant or garden bed) or a greenhouse. However, this will require you to lift (or open) the structure for a few hours daily (preferably in the morning) so pollinators can still get in and out. If you have a full schedule, this strategy can be challenging, so it's more of a temporary solution and a last resort.

Remember that pests only appear at a specific time of year, typically when the weather is warm and humid. Have a plan before an infestation occurs rather than trying to treat it when it's already in full swing. Besides that, you'll have to experiment and see what methods are effective and maintainable (given your resources and capabilities) and which need to be improved.

SOIL HEALTH AND MICROBES

We've all done that experiment in elementary school where you scoop up some soil and mix it with water. If you haven't (or you can't remember it), after mixing the dirt and sand and leaving it to settle for a week, there's a clear separation between the different types of soil: sand, silt, and clay. Sand will be the first layer at the bottom of the container, followed by a layer of silt, then clay, and any plant debris will float. But soil has much more going on than simply the different layers it likes to settle into.

Soil, together with water, sunlight, and air, creates the basis of plant life. Soil characteristics include physical, chemical, and biological interactions that all contribute to the decomposition of organic material, the cycle of nutrients, and carbon storage.

The physical elements of soil are the non-living components (the granules of sand, silt, and clay, along with decomposed plant and animal material and enzymes) that make up the structure of the soil. Meanwhile, the living components are microbes that spend most or all their lives underground (including fungi, bacteria, protozoa, and microbial enzymes).

The amount of living components in the soil controls the rate at which carbon is taken and released back into the soil (also known as the respiration rate). Soil with diverse biomass (living microorganisms) is more resilient to stressors like environmental change and disturbances. They can quickly return to the original, balanced state and activity after such stressors have occurred.

Underground life forms (microbial or otherwise) and their populations play a crucial role in the decomposition of organic matter. This participation means that microorganisms recycle nutrients through eating, digesting, and excreting dead plant and animal material so other plants can use them again. Less microbial activity means decomposition and respiration rates (and therefore nutrient cycling) occur slower and less efficiently, which can lead to a buildup of toxins and harmful bacteria.

The bottom line is that the living components in the soil contribute to the health of your garden. Microbial activity controls everything from the arrangements of the physical components (sand, silt, and clay) to the pH levels of your soil.

Soil Food Web

Soil biota refers to all the living components in soil, whether single-celled, microscopic, or visible to the naked eye. The underground community is diverse, and every member has a different (but necessary) role to keep the soil healthy. Fostering diversity in your soil and garden involves balancing predator and prey, establishing mutually beneficial relationships, and balance.

An imbalance of soil biota or lack of diversity can cause garden issues that require additional maintenance. This imbalance means that if your soil is unhealthy, your garden will only flourish once you do something about it on a foundational level.

The soil food web refers to exactly what you think it is: the circle of life in the soil. The following is a breakdown of all the life forms that reside on the Earth below your feet and the roles they play:

- Bacteria.

Bacteria come in many forms. It's more like an entire species with multiple branches of different kinds of bacteria. Some are good, and some are bad. But all of them are necessary for balance within the soil food web.

Bacteria fulfill many roles to ensure the soil stays healthy. Some bacteria produce and release enzymes that break down dead organic material into usable nutrients for plants. Others form mutually beneficial relationships with plant roots; they eat sugars that the roots release, and in exchange, the bacteria provide the plant with nitrogen. In soil with minimal exposure to oxygen and sunlight (deep underground or below bodies of water), a specific group of bacteria feeds on nitrogen, sulfur, hydrogen, and iron to ensure enough nutrients in the soil for the surrounding flora.

Then there's the group of harmful bacteria or pathogens. These little fellas cause your plants and their roots to fall ill (root rot, wilt, powdery mildew, dampening off, etc.) However, most beneficial or good bacteria will prey on or eat harmful bacteria. So, keeping the good bacteria populations high should be a top priority of any companion gardener.

Actinobacteria is another type of bacteria, but what sets them apart from regular bacteria is that they grow hyphae or root-like networks (much like fungi). You know that earthy smell when it rains or when you till the garden bed? You can thank actinobacteria for that!

- Fungi.

When most people hear "fungi," they immediately envision mushrooms. And that's true; fungi are mushrooms. Mushrooms are equivalent to fruits or flowers, and the spores are the seeds. But there's way more to it than just that. For starters, fungi can be single-celled or multicellular, and they grow hyphae, a mesh-like structure that can be so small they grow in between the cells of plant roots.

Often, the hyphae network of a mushroom is vast underneath the soil, and they grow around and into the roots of other plants. The main functions of fungi are decomposing organic material, controlling or regulating pests and diseases, and nutrient cycling. The hyphae can grow deep into the soil and transport minerals, nutrients, and water closer to the surface for plant roots to absorb.

Of course, some fungi do more harm than good and can infect your plants with diseases. But again, balance is the key.

- Protozoa.

Protozoa are single-celled, microscopic organisms that mainly serve as decomposers. They eat decaying matter and turn it into nitrogen, one of the main ingredients in fertilizer and compost (necessary for healthy soil and thriving crops).

- Nematodes.

These are tiny, roundworms. Most nematodes are microscopically small, but the largest nematode ever discovered and recorded was just over 26 feet long and living in the reproductive system of a sperm whale. However, you won't have to worry about coming across a nematode in your garden that is more significant than 2 to 5 mm.

Nematodes prey on all soil biota, such as bacteria and fungi (remember, even the good guys need a natural predator to keep the numbers balanced), but nematodes aren't the bad guys since they release nutrients into the soil. However, nematodes (much like all forms of life) can also be carriers of diseases.

- Earthworms.

By burrowing in the soil, earthworms manage to do something fundamental that microorganisms can't: they create space or air pockets. This function is essential because it's tough for roots to penetrate compacted soil. Compacted roots will result in stunted growth, disease, decreased plant vigor, and underperforming yields. Earthworms are like tilling machines but are less destructive and traumatic to the soil biota.

But besides allowing oxygen to reach the routes via the space they create, these slimy creatures travel deep into the Earth, eating as they go. On their way up, they expel their nutrient-rich "castings" closer to the top layer of soil, effectively mining precious food and nutrients for your plants to use up.

- Arthropods.

Millipedes, centipedes, springtails, and mites can invade your garden and wreak havoc on your crops. But they can also help break down organic matter and increase underground activity. Controlling populations of these pests can be advantageous. Like earthworms, they help aerate and mix the soil, which improves water retention while keeping the soil well-draining (well-draining soil doesn't mean zero water retention). They even feed on other types of potential soil pests, like nematodes.

The bottom line is that all living creatures on Earth (and within it) form part of the food web. And whenever the food chain is broken or unbalanced, bad things happen. The underground food web is no different. When specific populations grow out of control (even when the organisms are highly beneficial), the whole system falls apart, and the soil becomes infertile or uninhabitable.

That's why diversity is so important, especially in soil biota. Ironically, one way to foster a diverse underground food web is to diversify your crops. Crop rotation, intercropping, cover cropping, mulching, no-till systems, not using chemicals, and inoculating soil with mycorrhizal fungi can also encourage a balanced, healthy soil biota.

COMPANION PLANTING MYTHS AND MISCONCEPTIONS

Companion planting is a sought-after home or kitchen garden approach because it has many benefits. And as wonderful as it can be when done right, myths and misconceptions can't be managed once they've taken root (pun intended).

Here, we'll be debunking some common myths and misconceptions about companion planting so you have a better idea of what to expect and what it might be like in reality:

- The "Rules" Are Universal.

While it might be well-documented that certain plants benefit each other, there might still be a chance that that's not the case in your experience. You may plant marigolds with your tomatoes because they are said to ward off hornworms (a common tomato pest), only to be disappointed that it's not working in your garden.

Plants adapt to their environment over time. This adaptation might mean that specific genes or characteristics change and aren't universally applicable or consistent. While there are guidelines for companion planting, it always comes down to being willing to learn from your experiences and adapt your approach accordingly, even if it means going off-book.

- It Eliminates the Need for Pest Management.

Unless you're growing your garden in a sterile environment (in which case your crops won't thrive anyway), pests will always be present. The goal of companion planting has never been eliminating pests but managing their populations and, therefore, minimizing and maintaining their levels of destruction.

- It Prevents Plant Diseases.

A diverse garden can build the resilience and health of your garden and the soil in which they grow, but this doesn't mean diseases can't still break out. Companion planting and proper gardening hygiene practices can significantly lower the chances of your plants contracting a disease or illness—but the chances are never zero.

- It Is Always Successful.

Look, companion planting is better for your garden and the environment and can improve the quality of your yields and soil. You may fail on your initial attempt, and that's okay. Many things influence gardening, and the soil and climate conditions must be acceptable regardless of whether you're practicing companion planting.

Before planting anything, addressing issues such as soil health is essential. And even if the conditions are favorable, nature can be unpredictable. Companion planting is great for building a healthy and resilient garden, but that doesn't mean it will always withstand a harsh heatwave, raging storm, pest infestations, disease, or a significant temperature drop.

The science behind plant life and companion planting is astounding. So much is happening, and this chapter barely scratches the surface. Luckily, you don't need to know everything there is to learn to maintain a happy garden. The basics of plant chemistry will suffice.

3

PLANNING YOUR COMPANION GARDEN

Here it is, the moment you've been eagerly anticipating. Now, we're getting to the fun part: planning and designing your garden. In this chapter, we'll be going over how to approach planning your companion guilds to maximize the benefits and advantages of companion planting while also using all the available space.

One thing you should keep in mind is to prioritize function over beauty. You may want the marigolds in the front of your yard where everyone can see them, but if your front yard isn't getting enough sun, you need to use that space for shade-tolerant crops and flowers instead. A functional and thriving garden *looks* beautiful right from the planning stage.

YOUR GOALS

Your gardening goals will influence what crops you grow or what you do before you plant anything. Take a few minutes to think about what you want to accomplish with your garden. Maybe you want fresh herbs for cooking or brewing tea. You may only want to grow your favorite fruits and vegetables to lower your grocery bill. You may want a flower garden that attracts hummingbirds for you to look at.

While planning your garden has a lot to do with your style and preference, here are a few more things to consider:

- Soil Quality.

You can buy DIY kits to test soil quality at most garden stores or send a sample to a lab for more accurate and detailed results. Either way, knowing the current state of your soil is always a good starting point. A top priority goal should be to improve the health of your soil in perpetuity, meaning that you're replacing nutrients (following permaculture gardening practices) as much as you can and not just stripping the soil. In a later chapter, we'll discuss how to improve the health and fertility of your soil.

- Harvest.

Please list all the herbs, fruits, and vegetables you want to grow for harvesting and consumption. Only add crops to this list that you will use wisely and estimate how much you'll need to cultivate based on how frequently you eat it. If you only eat tomatoes once a month, you don't need five tomato plants. If you don't like onions, don't grow them (unless you're growing them for pest management). If you want to pickle or conserve some of your crops and have them fresh, you'll need to produce more.

It would help if you also considered the specific climate you're in. You can only grow pineapples in Canada with special precautions like building a greenhouse and purchasing UV lamps. To make things easier, choose your crops from a trusted online source that lists what grows best in your state, region, or country.

- Pest Control.

Research the types of crops and flowers you want to grow in your garden (as per the previous point) and know what pests are most common for those specifically. Doing so will provide you with a list of potential future pests. You can narrow this list by looking into which pests occur more frequently or abundantly in your climate or area.

You now (hopefully) have a shortened list of pests to worry about. Use this list and look up herbs or crops that repel these pests and add them to your list of crops you want to plant. This second list is non-negotiable. Even if you don't wish to have fennel in your garden or don't like the taste of it, it's a small sacrifice you need to make to keep aphids at bay. Dry it and give it to your grand-mother, or use it as mulch at the end of the season. There's always a way to get as much use out of what you have, even if you didn't want it in the first place.

Your goals might be simple: Improve soil quality, grow food, eat food, repeat. Or you might have more elaborate plans like growing a community food forest (if you have the space for it) or saving the seeds. Nevertheless, you need to know what those goals are and break down the steps you need to take to accomplish them.

GUILD PLANNING

A guild is a small community of plants (in a small or medium garden bed or container) that work well together. By this, I mean every type of crop supports the growth and well-being of the other crops in the guild. You must fulfill three prominent roles in a guild that contribute to the overall success of the harvest: attract, repel, and cover.

To elaborate: In every guild, you need a crop that attracts pollinators for bigger harvests. Repels pests by either attracting predatory insects or exuding a powerful scent. It covers the ground, suppressing weeds and improving soil quality and structure.

Furthermore, a guild usually has one primary crop. This crop is either the biggest or has the most prominent fruits or the crop you use the most. An apple tree, for instance, is the center of the guild, and you can plant many things underneath it (but the tree is the main crop). Tomatoes are another excellent example; they only do a little for the guild itself and don't take up much space, but they're a staple in many kitchens.

Nutrient cycling aids or fertilizing plants are another aspect to consider. Most annual crops are heavy feeders and take much out of the soil, so you need nitrogen fixers to keep the soil healthy and fertile (legumes are excellent nitrogen fixers). However, legumes are only good companions for some of your other crops. You need an alternative if legumes aren't good companions for a specific crop type. The fix could be adding a plant to the guild that brings nutrients to the surface (a taproot) or topping the soil with compost more often.

Planning a guild can be complicated and requires significant creative problem-solving skills and intense research. Remember how much space all your crops will take up at maturity, both above and below ground (remember, the roots also need space). You need to consider sun, water, and soil requirements, which affect the layout of your garden. Even plants that are tried and tested companions may have slightly different needs, but it's usually not enough to interfere with the growth or production of each other, so it still works.

Some plants are the opposite of companions. Either they will die or kill each other if you plant them nearby (due to those VOCs we talked about), or their requirements are so different that you can't possibly accommodate both of them in the same space. Hence, more often than not, you'll need to plan multiple guilds to grow everything you want to grow.

For example, if you want to grow blueberries and cauliflower, they must be developed in separate guilds because they have different soil pH requirements. Blueberries like acidic soil, but cauliflower prefers alkaline soil; neither of these crops will thrive if you disregard entirely their pH needs.

Popular Guild Combinations

If you're still getting your feet wet with the companion planting thing, researching and putting together all the information to develop your guild can be overwhelming. It's better to start with one or two beginner guilds until you

become familiar with the process. I assembled a list of typical guilds that are highly likely to succeed since they've been well-documented and replicated by many home gardeners. You'll still need to research when you should propagate them, sun requirements, water needs, soil preference, etc. But for the most part, here are some beginner guilds that will likely do well:

- Tomatoes, basil, garlic, and marigold.
- Green beans, radish, celery, and nasturtium.
- Carrots, onions, rosemary, and leeks.
- Lettuce, mint, beets, and marigold.
- Squash, peas, dill, and marigold.
- Sweet corn, cucumber, beans, and borage.
- Potatoes, horseradish, cabbage, and marigold.

- Strawberries, spinach, chives, and alyssum.
- Blueberries, lemon balm, borage, and azaleas.
- Melon (of any kind), broccoli, garlic, and lavender.
- Capsicums (bell peppers, chilies, etc.), pumpkin, lettuce, and echinacea.
- Eggplant, potato, parsley, and marigold.

If you're not keen on mulching your garden bed every so often, try living mulch. Living mulch is low-growing (or ground-covering) crops you grow wherever the soil is exposed or between crops. Some good choices for living mulch are borage, creeping thyme, clover (a nitrogen fixer), dandelion, and yarrow. But you can also use other low-growing crops as living mulch, for example, chives, chamomile, chickweed, mustard, parsley, and even strawberries. Ensure your ground cover crops are compatible with all the other crops in that guild.

Incompatible Crops

There are many reasons why certain crops are incompatible with each other. The three main reasons why some plants don't get along are: a crop releases a chemical that kills or, at the very least, stunts the growth of another plant. They compete for the same nutrients. Or they attract the same pests (which could lead to an infestation).

As a general rule, you should avoid planting too many crops of the same family together in one guild (choose either garlic or chives, but not both, for example). But to make things easier for you, here is a list of common crops and what you should avoid putting with them in the same guild:

- Asparagus: Avoid planting with alliums (onion family), potatoes, and fennel.
- Beans (or legumes): Avoid planting with brassicas and alliums.
- Beets: Avoid planting with legumes or mustard.
- Brassicas: Avoid planting with legumes, tomatoes, lettuce, and strawberries.
- Carrots: Avoid planting with dill, fennel, or parsnips.
- Corn: Avoid planting with tomatoes.
- Cucumber: Avoid planting with melons (of any kind), potatoes, and sage.
- Fennel: Plant in pots or containers away from your crops since this herb can be very picky and incompatible with many crops. It's just easier to plant it completely separately (if you want it) instead of trying to include it somewhere.
- Lettuce: Avoid planting with brassicas.
- Peas: Avoid planting with alliums.
- Peppers: Avoid planting with brassicas and fennel.
- Potatoes: Avoid planting with brassicas, tomatoes, carrots, cucumbers, gourds, fennel, and asparagus.
- Pumpkins: Avoid planting with root crops (beets, onions, potatoes, carrots, radishes, etc.)
- Strawberries: Avoid planting with brassicas and fennel.
- Tomatoes: Avoid planting with brassicas, corn, dill, fennel, and other nightshades (peppers, eggplant, potatoes).

Always double-check from several sources whether all the crops in your guilds are compatible during the planning stage. Yes, it's a lot of research, but I promise it's necessary and worth it.

DESIGN AND LAYOUT

There's a lot to consider when planning not only your guilds but the actual layout of those guilds within your available space. The two most critical factors in designing a layout in your garden are space and light requirements. Most garden fruiting crops require full sun (6-8 hours per day), while some may benefit from afternoon shade (or will grow just fine in partial sun).

You need to know the sun requirements of all your selected plants and how much space they will take up once they mature. If you have minimal space available for a garden, you need to grow your guilds in containers or pots. If you have a large shade area, you must factor this in when choosing crops and designing layouts for your guilds.

Spend some time in your gardening space and map out where the sunny and shady spots are throughout the day. In addition, you should measure your space to accurately determine how big your guilds should be and make a garden blueprint to scale. Another thing to consider when designing your garden is water accessibility, though this is usually only a problem with larger gardening spaces.

There are a few approaches you can choose from when planning your guilds and their layouts in your space, for example:

- Blocks.

Divide your space into four squares and assign each square a guild. This approach doesn't mean the whole square should be a garden bed; it just means space is specifically for a particular guild.

This method ensures that you will receive four guilds without fail. An example of using this approach is: You plan out and divide your entire space into four squares. Square one is for guild one: Tomatoes, basil, garlic, and marigolds, for example. If square one is too big to make into a singular garden bed, you can further divide square one into multiple garden beds (with dividing footpaths in between for easy access from all sides). So now you have numerous smaller garden beds within an allocated square, and each garden bed within this space contains a guild consisting of a tomato, basil, and marigold plant, with a few garlic bulbs.

Repeat this for each of the four squares (or more if you have the space) with a different guild. Remember, the size of the crops will dictate how big your garden beds should be. But you should be able to reach all sides of the garden bed comfortably (by making it narrow enough if it's against a wall or has a path around it while still accessing the center).

The advantage of this approach is that you're way less likely to lose your entire guild and harvest to pest infestations, diseases, and so on. However, it could be more space-efficient.

- Rectangles.

With this method, you can use the classic gardening layout of planting rows (essentially slim rectangular garden beds). However, in nature, you never see crops growing in perfect rows, but whether or not there's a good, scientific reason for that (other than it being random) is still up for debate. If you plan on using rows for your guilds, make sure taller crops aren't casting shadows over the low-growing ones.

Alternatively, you can make as many large-ish rectangular garden beds (raised or otherwise) as you can fit into your space and assign a different guild to each one. This way (using the previous example), one rectangle has multiple tomato, basil, onion, and marigold plants—so you have one large guild instead of separating them like in the square approach (previous bullet point).

Remember to include footpaths between the rectangular garden beds and ensure you can reach every inch without slipping a disk in your back. This method's main "selling point" is that it makes good use of all available space, especially if space is limited. But the downside of having an entire guild in one garden bed is that pests and diseases might get to all of them before you can intervene.

- Square Foot.

For this method, you will make as many one-square-foot garden beds comfortably fit into your space (with narrow footpaths in between). From here, you can plant one to three plants in each bed (depending on how much space the crop needs). You can make each bed a tiny guild if they will all fit or plant the companion crops in neighboring beds.

This method is also a great space saver. Suppose you can only plant your crops directly. In that case, you can also grow your garden in a series of large containers (approximately one square foot in size or diameter), put the crops in the same guild, and separate them from the others.

- Vertical.

Vertical gardening takes home first prize when maximizing space in scenarios where you don't have space to spare, live in an apartment with only a tiny balcony for outside space, or barely have any yard to play with. This approach includes vertical planters, but you can also grow quite a lot in hanging baskets, metal shelves, or against trellises.

The only downside to vertical gardens (or any gardens not grown in the ground directly, such as container gardens or raised garden beds on concrete) is that they need watering more often.

SOIL PREPARATION

You have thoroughly researched every crop and flower you plan to cultivate in your garden. You know the specific requirements of each plant, where to place them, and how to layout your garden to maximize their growth. You've researched every crop and flower in every plant guild you plan to cultivate into oblivion. You know what makes them tick, what they need, where you will put them, and how you'll lay them out in your garden. What's next?

Your garden is only as good as your soil. Soil serves as both a literal and figurative foundation for your garden. There's no way around it; you need to know what's happening with your soil and whether there's anything to fix or be worried about. Luckily, you can learn quite a lot about the health and well-being of your soil with a few easy DIY tests.

But before we get into that, you can test your soil by sending a sample to your local county extension office, which is usually inexpensive or completely free. Professional tests are much more comprehensive since they test pH levels, soil texture, type, and amounts of available nutrients. They will also give you specific advice on what to do to correct any potential problems.

However, there are many ways you can test your soil without having to collect a sample, send it off, and then patiently wait for the results to come back. These home tests are way less accurate, but they will give you something to work with if professional tests are only an option after some time.

Testing Soil pH Levels

Most garden crops prefer neutral soil (between six and seven). Of course, some crops prefer either extreme (more acidic or alkaline soil), but that's the exception and not the rule. A neutral soil pH level likely means your soil is relatively healthy, and you won't need to do much concerning preparation for planting other than ensuring the soil stays healthy and fertile.

The problem with an unbalanced soil pH level (lower than six or higher than seven) is that there might be enough nutrients in the soil, but the plants can't absorb them properly. This results in the crops dying from a nutrient deficiency even though there's plenty of it to go around.

You can buy home test kits for testing soil pH levels (try your local gardening center or store). With the help of technology, we now have handy-dandy gadgets like pH meters that can test your soil's pH by simply pushing some prongs into the ground and getting immediate results—these devices are reusable, too!

I advise regularly testing your soil's pH levels every two years. The best time to test the pH levels is in the fall after the crops have died down; this will also give you some time to rectify any issues so your soil is ready to go when spring arrives.

Neutralizing Soil pH Levels

You'll be pleased to hear that solving a pH problem does not require a Ph.D. It's pretty simple. If your soil's pH level is below six, add garden lime, wood ash, or mushroom compost to your garden beds. If the pH level is higher than seven, you can add sulfur and compost.

Either way, you want to do this a few months before planting anything in the soil. It can take weeks for the pH levels to stabilize after corrective treatments. Test the pH levels every couple of weeks initially to ensure things are going in the right direction. Remember to mulch your garden beds after a neutralizing treatment and be patient.

Testing Soil Type

Generally, healthy soil contains around 40% silt, 40% sand, and 20% clay. Do you remember that test we discussed earlier that you performed in elementary school, where you mix soil with water and let it settle to see the layers? Determining your soil type at home is precisely that experiment, only more detailed and with additional steps.

You'll need a glass jar (a Mason or clear plastic jar will do) with a lid, a ruler, and a timer. Dig a hole about six inches deep into the soil of the area you want to use for gardening and fill the jar halfway with the dirt you just dug up; try to avoid collecting plant matter like grass, leaves, or weeds.

Fill your jar with dirt and add water until absorbed. Close the container and shake vigorously for three minutes. Place the jar down on a level surface and start the timer. After one minute, measure how much sediment has collected at the bottom with the ruler. This measurement is the amount of sand in your soil.

After four minutes, measure the sediment level again. The difference between the two measurements is the amount of silt in your soil. (If your first measurement was an inch, for example, and the second measurement was an inch and a half, the difference is half an inch.)

Now, go about your day and check back in with your mud jar in 24 hours. Measure the sediment again and calculate the difference between the second and third measurements. This figure is the amount of clay in your soil. (For example, Your second measurement was an inch and a half; after 24 hours, it's two inches. The difference is half an inch).

You can eyeball it; you don't have to whip out a calculator. The first two measurements should be equal. This equality means that the ratios line up nicely if you get an inch of sediment after a minute and there are about two inches after four minutes. The third measurement should be half of the first (half an inch based on our previous example).

Fixing the Ratios

Based on the test results, you can calculate whether you have loamy soil (40-40-20 ratio), sandy soil, or clay soil. Loamy soil is the golden ratio, in which case you don't have to do much of anything—sprinkle some compost, add a layer of mulch, and call it a day until you're ready to plant.

If you have more sandy soil, you can mix hummus, aged manure, peat moss, or sawdust into your garden bed (you can also try sourcing clay-type soil from somewhere and incorporating it into your garden bed). If you have soil with a lot of clay, add coarse sand, compost, and peat moss. And remember to mulch!

Testing General Soil Health

The easiest and most accurate way to determine whether your soil is healthy without lab tests is to check for life. Granted, you won't be able to see many of the life forms in your soil since they're microscopic. However, you can see earthworms and check if your soil has them.

Earthworms will only go anywhere near soil with enough organic matter or nutrients to sustain them. If there are enough earthworms in the soil you want to use for planting, there's a perfect chance your soil has everything it needs to support your crops.

You'll only need a shovel, a large piece of cardboard, and the right timing to perform the earthworm test. The best time to check for earthworms is in the middle of spring, and after it has rained, you can also hose down the area thoroughly and wait a day or so before performing the test.

Lay out your cardboard and dig precisely one cubic foot of soil out of your garden, throwing all the soil you dig up onto the cardboard. Look through the excavated dirt for earthworms and count how many there are (you can throw them back into the hole as you find them). Healthy, fertile soil will have at least ten earthworms per one cubic foot of soil.

Improving Soil Health

If you find less than ten earthworms or none in the soil sample, your soil needs organic matter. You can rectify this by gently mixing in compost, aged manure, or leaf mold into the top layer of soil. Adding a generous layer of mulch will also keep the soil moist and create an environment where microorganisms break down the compost and manure to release the nutrients quickly. The mulch will also break down over time, adding to the amount of organic matter available in the soil, which will also incentivize earthworms to come set up camp!

SEASONAL PLANNING

A decent portion of your crops will be annuals that you'll have to re-sow yearly. You need to know which plants stay long-term (perennials) and which ones are just visiting (annuals). As you know, there are different crops for every season. If you want to grow crops only some of the year, you should plant ground cover crops in the off seasons or at least cover your soil with a thick layer of mulch. This tactic will prevent soil erosion and keep the soil fertile.

This example brings us to two significant things you must remember when practicing companion planting and designing your guilds and layout: Crop rotation and succession planting.

Crop Rotation

Crop rotation refers to changing your garden layout so you're not indefinitely growing crops in the same garden bed. You should rotate your crops every other year for a typical home garden. But why?

There are three main reasons (or benefits if you want to look at it that way) as to why crop rotation is so important:

- To Replenish Nutrients.

Every type of crop requires a different ratio of nutrients. Crop rotation allows the soil to bring all the lost nutrients to equilibrium, so it never loses fertility. Of course, you'll need to aid in the general rejuvenation of nutrients by adding compost every so often.

- To Reduce Diseases.

Soil-borne diseases feed on specific plants and crops (like early blight and powdery mildew, for example). When you move the crops around from time to time, you essentially remove the host from the equation, meaning disease populations don't build up in the soil over time (which will blindsight you and destroy an entire guild or crop type).

- To Confuse Pests.

Crop rotation won't eradicate a pest problem or prevent it. Interrupting pest life cycles will slow population growth, making it easier to manage with natural pest control methods.

When implementing crop rotation correctly and successfully, the most important thing to remember is crop "families." When it's time to rotate crops, avoid planting anything related to the previous guild in the same area. For example, if you have been growing cucumbers (in the Cucurbit family) in one of your garden beds for the past two years, you shouldn't rotate with any other crops from the Cucurbit family (or guilds that have them as a member).

You should know which family your crops belong to and plan your guilds around it so it's easier to rotate them. So, here's a list of crop families based on what most home gardeners tend to grow in their backyards:

- Alliums: Onions (including green onions), shallots, scallions, garlic, chives, and leeks.
- Brassicas: Broccoli, cauliflower, cabbage, Brussels sprouts, kale, turnips, radishes (including horseradish), mustard greens, bok choy, and arugula.

- Cucurbits (gourds): Cucumbers, zucchini, all pumpkins and squash, and all melons.
- Legumes: All beans, peas (including cowpeas and chickpeas), lentils, soybeans, alfalfa, clovers, vicia, and peanuts.
- Nightshades: Eggplants, tomatoes, potatoes (including sweet potatoes), and capsicums (all peppers and chilies).
- Umbellifers: Carrots, celery, cumin, fennel, parsnips, parsley, dill, and cilantro.

It's important to note that you don't have to rotate your perennial crops since they take much less soil nutrients than quick-growing annuals.

Keeping track of which guilds to rotate and where to move them can be tricky. Color coding your guilds (and even individual plants) might help. Make each family a different color and try to keep relatives and cousins together (avoid placing a member of the allium family in more than one or two guilds, for example).

A simple way to keep track of which guilds you're growing where is to keep the sketch you make (when designing your garden space) until you need to rotate your crops and plan your rotation according to that.

In some cases, it might be impossible to rotate your crops, like if you have limited space. If this is your situation, you can get around it by supplementing the soil with compost and organic fertilizer more often than usual and letting the soil rest every winter (or for a whole year after three to five years of continuous planting). Remember the nitrogen-fixing cover crops; this is essential if you can't rotate.

Succession Planting

In agriculture, succession planting refers to timing your crop propagation or plantings to extend the harvesting period and reduce waste (due to abundance). It also allows you to maximize space in a miniature garden to get the most out of it.

Succession planting is not so much necessary for companion planting as it is a "pro tip." This gardening technique is typically employed only on crops that complete their life cycle within a year. But why should you do this? The main benefits of succession planting are that it utilizes space more efficiently, provides fresh produce for longer, and allows you to grow a more extensive variety of crops in a small space.

Let me explain: When you propagate or sow all your seeds at once, the fruit will all be ready for harvest within a short time frame. This method means you'll have fresh produce for a couple of weeks once they're ripe and nothing for an entire year.

Many home gardeners will preserve their produce by pickling, conserving, or freezing the abundance so they can consume it later and let nothing go to waste. Don't get me wrong, I love a good strawberry jam or pickled onion. But frozen fruits and vegetables and dried herbs just don't hit the spot like fresh ones, not to mention all the prep work that goes into preserving all the harvested produce.

Succession planting is relatively straightforward, but it is gratifying. All you must do is start propagating a few seeds indoors before the specific planting season arrives, waiting a few days or weeks and bearing a few more. The exact time frame for staggering your crops will differ based on how long a specific crop germinates or matures.

By starting your crops earlier and staggering their planting, their maturity rate will differ, which means you can have fresh produce very early in the season and up to the end or beyond.

To break it down even more, this is what you do:

Depending on how early you want to produce ready for harvest and how long it takes to mature and bear fruit, you can calculate how early you should start propagating your seeds indoors.

For example, tomatoes can take up to 16 weeks before the fruit matures. If you want tomatoes prepared for harvest earlier in the season, you should start propagating a plant or two (based on how many you want to have) every other week at least two months in advance. Start planting tomatoes (a summer crop) indoors in the middle of spring. By summer, they'll be ready to transplant with only a few more weeks before they start flowering and producing fruit.

Regarding how succession planting saves space, it's pretty simple: Annuals typically die after they've set fruit. This thinking means that when one plant has finished fruiting and starts to wither, you can immediately replace it with a younger plant instead of leaving the space barren.

Keep in mind the latest recommended sowing time. Propagating or sowing past this date won't benefit you much as the plant will likely die before the fruit is ready for harvest anyway. For quick-growing crops like radish (which you can harvest in as little as three weeks), propagate two weeks in advance and closer together every three days or so. But realistically, how much radish are you going to use? Be mindful when deciding how many plants you want to grow for each crop.

Planning a garden based on companions and guilds entails a lot of thought and research. Still, once you've figured it out, everything is much easier, from general maintenance to pest management, weed control, and soil health. Please take advantage of the planning because your garden will show its appreciation!

4

COMPANION PLANTING — VEGETABLES

"Double the yield, not the work." That's what I always say. And believe it or not, it's possible; I know because that's what I've been doing for many years. The subject of this chapter is fundamental pairings for vegetable guilds. Keyword: Pair. As in simple but effective guilds that only include two types of crops with a focus on veggies.

These simple, classic guilds are beginner-friendly and true space savers, perfect for those who want to try their hand at companion planting first and those who have limited space (but still want to grow *something*.)

CLASSIC VEGETABLE PLANT PAIRINGS

A guild doesn't have to be a collection of several different crop types; the "poly" in polyculture means more than one. So, even if you grow two types of crops that complement each other, you're not cultivating a monoculture anymore, which is a good thing!

I've selected these vegetable pairings because they work as is and don't require you to plant anything else. Everyone can grow them regardless of skill and experience. They can also work in multiple situations: Container gardening, raised garden beds, little space, or lots of space. You can quickly scale these guilds up; if you want a more significant yield, you can plant more than one of each crop type within the pairing (four pepper plants instead of one, for instance).

We'll also review each pairing's benefits, special planting and care instructions, pest and disease management, harvesting tips, and considerations so you know exactly how to take care of your guilds.

Basil and Tomato

Basil and tomatoes are soulmates. They taste phenomenal together in a hearty dish and can also be considered best friends in the soil. Although tomato plants require a lot of nutrients to grow plump and juicy fruit, basil is a light feeder. Which means they don't compete for nutrients in the soil. But that is just the tip of the iceberg regarding how these two crops benefit each other.

Benefits

Basil is the companion who pulls most of the weight in this pairing. Not only does basil repel common tomato pests (hornworms, whiteflies, aphids, and thrips), but it also deters any mosquitos and flies in the vicinity. This deterrence means your time spent around this companion pairing will be much more pleasant. Basil also aids in tomato plants' root growth, size, and general production.

Tomato brings one significant benefit: the leaves protect basil from the harsh sun while shading the soil so less moisture evaporates. Add a layer of mulch to the equation, and your basil and tomato guild will never go thirsty.

Many gardeners swear that basil also enhances the flavor profile of tomatoes. When used together in a dish, this is the case. However, there is no scientific proof to back up the claim that pairing basil with tomatoes in the garden enhances the flavor of the tomato by itself.

Care and Maintenance

Tomatoes grow best when the soil reaches a temperature of 60°F. If you're implementing succession planting, you must propagate your tomatoes indoors until the soil has warmed up enough at the start of summer.

Use well-draining soil; this is a general rule of thumb as 99% of crops need moist but not wet soil, or else, they can dampen off or develop root rot. As mentioned, tomatoes love lots of direct sun, so situate your guild in a spot that receives full sun (at least six hours a day). You'll also need to build or supply some trellis or support for your tomatoes; otherwise, the plant will not be able to support the weight of the fruit (tomatoes touching the ground will result in them getting squishy, rotten, or bursting open).

Basil germinates and matures very quickly. Once your tomatoes are ready to be transplanted, sow four or five basil seeds around your tomato plants (about 12 inches from the base of the tomato plant). As the basil starts sprouting, thin the seedlings (remove the smallest ones) until there are about two basil plants around every tomato plant if you're planting them in a garden bed. When planting them in containers, only one basil plant per tomato plant (depending on the container size or pot). The basil plants will start providing full-blown benefits within a few weeks.

If you are growing basil and tomatoes in separate pots or containers, you can still have them benefit each other by placing them right next to each other.

Harvesting

Tomatoes are ripe and ready for harvesting when they break away from the plant with a gentle twist. This time is usually when the tomatoes are completely red and have a slight give when squeezing them (as opposed to being extremely firm). However, tomatoes can be ripe and not entirely red, which could be because the tomato plant didn't receive enough sunlight. You *can* pick tomatoes with green spots, but store them indoors with the stem side down for a few days or until they turn red.

You can harvest basil at any time, but if you want the best flavor from your basil, pinch leaves off the top of a few stems in the morning right after the dew has evaporated.

Carrots and Onions

Root crops, in general, are great for your garden because they help aerate and essentially till the soil, preventing impaction and improving soil health. Even though carrots and onions are both root crops, they make for very effective pairings and can stand independently as a guild (though you will need to protect the soil with mulch). Since both carrots and beets are root vegetables, it is advisable to plant them at a distance from each other to avoid any potential competition for nutrients and space.

You can plant carrots with any onion; it doesn't have to be the classic white bulbous onion in the grocery store. For example, you can pair carrots with spring onions, shallots, red onions, chives, garlic, and radishes. You'll still get the full spectrum of benefits by growing carrots and any allium together.

Benefits

Speaking of which, the most notable benefit of a carrot and onion companion pair is pest management. Usually, only one plant supplies the remaining guild with pest-repellent properties. Like in the case of tomatoes and basil, the basil repels tomato pests, but the tomato does nothing to keep slugs from munching on basil leaves at night.

The imbalance is different here. The pungent alliums do an excellent job of repelling carrot flies, while carrots return the favor by keeping onion flies at bay. Besides preventing soil compaction, leaving a couple of onions and carrots in the soil to decompose after the season has passed can improve soil fertility. When root vegetables break down, they release nutrients, particularly phosphorus, into the soil. This process also leads to an increase in organic matter, which helps to boost the populations of beneficial microorganisms in the soil. Nutrient cycling ends up being more efficient as a result.

Care and Maintenance

For crops grown for their fruit, vegetables, or roots, it is advisable to use well-draining soil and ensure they receive full sun. In addition, you should water onions and carrots regularly when they're young (at least one inch every week) and avoid watering them overhead; instead, water them at the base.

Something to remember when planting onions and carrots together is that while they thrive as companions, they need their personal space. The spacing will vary depending on how big your onion and carrot varieties are (spring onions and chives will be fine if planted three or four inches from carrots, while the classic onion needs more space, so go with four to six inches instead).

You should leave enough space between carrots and onions to avoid accidentally pulling up neighboring carrots that still need to be harvested. Carrots don't do well when disrupted, so even if you replant a carrot, it will likely stop growing and start to decompose.

Remember to sow carrot seeds directly into the place you want them to mature since transplanting young carrots will disrupt them, and they will not fare well after the fact (that's if they survive at all). Carrots prefer cooler weather (they are winter crops, after all), which also makes them sweeter, which is why you should start sowing them in spring, about three weeks before the last frost is due (and again a couple weeks later if you're implementing succession planting).

Onions are pretty chill and don't need many precautions regarding care and maintenance. Cut off any flower "spikes" that appear so all the plant's attention is directed to growing the root (the part you want) instead of the flowers. Stop watering onions when the leaves start to sag.

Harvesting

Carrots and onions mature at the same rate (depending on the variety of carrots and onions you grow) and are typically ready to harvest three to four months after sowing. However, before you gather your entire yield of carrots, first harvest one and taste it; they should be sweet, crisp, and crunchy.

Bulb onions are ready to harvest once the stalks and leaves topple over (you'll see a noticeable bend close to the base of the onion plant) and start to turn brown. Grass-like onions (like spring onions and chives) are ready to use when they reach about eight inches in height.

Ensure you note the sowing dates when planting successively, so you only harvest these younger crops after they're ready.

Peppers and Marigold

Marigolds are always a safe bet if you need help deciding what to pair crops with because they get along with virtually every plant you can think of. When in doubt, marigold is the answer! They benefit your garden in many ways, and the flowers are also edible. Peppers include the entire capsicum family, from the flavorful bell peppers to the spicy jalapenos.

Benefits

This pairing is another tomato and basil situation where the peppers benefit more from the marigolds than vice versa. But since we love peppers so much, we let it slide. As mentioned, marigolds help your garden in many ways, including attracting pollinators, which means better yields. Along with bees, it also attracts predatory insects (like lacewings, ladybugs, hoverflies, and wasps), which feed on common garden pests that enjoy your peppers' spiciness.

Another unorthodox method of using marigolds for pest management is growing them into a sacrificial (or trap) crop. Weevils and beetles would much rather feast on marigolds than peppers.

Marigolds can also help control specific nematode populations, specifically those that cause root rot. And the strong scent of marigolds might help hide the smell of your peppers from pests, like a last resort. If all else fails, at least the pests will have a tough time figuring out where to go.

Care and Maintenance

Both marigolds and capsicums are sun lovers, so ensure they get six to eight hours of sun daily. Marigolds prefer it if the soil has time to dry between watering. Check the soil once a week by sticking your finger an inch or so into it; if the soil feels dry and very little is sticking to your finger, it's time to water it (otherwise, wait another day or so). Water them at the base; marigolds prefer to keep their leaves dry.

Marigolds are annuals but tend to reseed readily, so you'll find new ones pop up the following year. It sounds counterintuitive, but if you want your marigolds to flower for longer, frequently cut off dead or withering flowers, and new ones will grow in the same season! This process is called deadheading.

Capsicums like moist soil, so you must water your peppers more frequently than your marigolds. If your marigold and peppers are in the same garden bed or container, water around the base of the peppers twice a week and around the marigolds only once a week or so. Yes, there will be some water distribution, but if you space them correctly, this should be fine. It would help if you spaced marigolds and peppers at least twelve inches apart.

Aerate and fertilize the soil by mixing in mulching material and compost before sowing or transplanting, in addition to a layer of mulch on top. To feed your peppers (heavy feeders), sprinkle a generous layer of compost followed by more mulch at least once during the flowering period. This pair will benefit from crop rotation as well.

Harvesting

To harvest marigold flowers, cut them off to your desired stem length.

Harvesting capsicums are also relatively straightforward. You can harvest green bell peppers or chilies once they're big enough or wait to turn yellow or red. Fun fact: There are no color variations of peppers; they all start green and change to different colors (yellow or red) by being left on the plant for longer. Peppers might not come off the plant as efficiently as ripe tomatoes do, so to prevent damaging the plant, use gardening shears or pruners to cut them off their stems when harvesting.

Corn, Beans, and Squash (The Three Sisters)

The Three Sisters guild is an ancient, prevalent one that dates back to the 16th century. Native Americans made good use of this guild and have passed it down for generations. This trio is companion planting at its finest, and you'll see why.

Benefits

Corn, beans, and squash look after each other like family (hence the name "Three Sisters"). For starters, the corn serves as much-needed support for the climbing beans (a natural trellis, if you will). Beans, as we know, are nitrogen fixers that keep the soil fertile so the other two sisters can thrive. The leaves of the squash plant act as a natural covering for the soil, preventing weed growth and maintaining moisture and coolness. But squash leaves are also prickly, which helps keep more significant pests away (like raccoons and rabbits).

Care and Maintenance

Tending to your soil before planting anything is always advisable, but this is especially true when growing the Three Sisters. Besides primary soil care (adjusting pH levels, adding compost, and mulching), for the Three Sisters guild, you'll need to create mounds. Each mound should be at least a foot high and 3 feet in diameter and spaced 4 feet apart (if you're growing multiple Three Sister guilds). It would help if you flattened the mounds at the top to create a surface area of at least 2 feet in diameter.

Planting corn on the flattened part first and in the middle of the mound would be best. Sow four to six kernels (any more than this, and you risk overcrowding). You can make two or three one-inch-deep holes spaced apart evenly and place two corn kernels in each hole. If both kernels germinate in a single hole, you'll have to thin out the smallest since corn can't grow that close to each other.

Once the corn reaches around six inches in height, you can plant the pole beans (about four bean plants per mound, spaced evenly along the base of the corn). Wait another week before sowing six squash seeds around the mound's perimeter, again spaced evenly apart.

Planting small-leafed squash such as zucchini or Hubbard would be best since more significant squash variants will be too big and heavy for this guild. And the beans you choose should be climbers (not bush beans) but not vigorously so. However, you can use any variety of corn.

The squash leaves are only sometimes the best deterrent for more minor pests. If you want to add another layer of protection on the pest control front, plant a few marigolds between your squash or in front of them all around your mound (keep spacing in mind). It might be worth making some platforms for your squash to sit on (you can use grid wire to make a cube to lift it off the ground); if they're touching the ground, they might develop soft spots or go rotten.

Harvesting

You can tell that corn is ready for harvesting when the kernels are plump and release a creamy liquid when you press your fingernail into them unless you are growing a hard-kernelled variety like popcorn. Usually, this is around six weeks after the ear first appears on the stalk. To harvest, firmly hold the ear of corn, pull it downwards, and twist (you can leave the husk on until you're ready to cook it); it should break off relatively easily.

With pole beans (or any other climbing beans), the most crucial thing when harvesting is not waiting until the bean pods swell and the beans inside the pod reach maturity. Most beans are ready to be harvested about two months after sowing, but they will continue to produce more beans until winter is on your doorstep. Beans tend to snap off the plant with minimal effort.

Squash is ready to be harvested when it is firm, the rind is the correct color (based on the type of squash you're growing), and the stem is dry. This maturity typically takes two to four months from the time of sowing. Harvesting squash is simple; you can twist them off or use pruners to cut them off the vine if they're stubborn.

Spinach and Beets

These two vegetables bond over their love for cool weather. Spinach and beets complement each other beautifully. Spinach has shallow roots but will develop a taproot once it's mature, bringing nutrients from further down in the soil to the surface for the hungry, heavy-feeding beets to enjoy. And even though beets are a root vegetable, their roots are still shallow compared to a mature spinach's. This difference is perfect because these two crops won't compete for underground space either.

Benefits

Beets (just like any other root vegetable) are great for keeping soil aerated and preventing impaction. The leaves of beets are big and nutritious, which you can use as mulching materials to improve soil fertility or in a salad.

Similarly, spinach also serves as a living mulch, suppressing weeds and shading the ground to protect it from the harsh sun. However, you might have to supplement this guild pairing with a third party regarding pest management.

But while weeds or ground cover might not be an issue, spinach and beets attract various leaf-eating insects, aphids, spider mites, slugs, and snails. You can grow nasturtiums as a trap crop for aphids that love beetroot, zinnias repel certain spinach-dwelling pests, or opt for parsley to attract predatory insects.

Care and Maintenance

Spinach grows best in full sun but might benefit from partial or afternoon shade in warmer climates. Prepare the soil before sowing spinach by lightly spading in compost or aged manure into the top layer of soil. To prevent bolting (early flowering), under-production, or wilting of spinach leaves in hot weather, water lightly several times per week instead of watering heavily once per week (spinach is not drought-tolerant).

You can sow spinach seeds directly in the soil or germinate them indoors and transplant them later (especially useful if you're implementing succession planting). Nevertheless, spinach is a cool-weather crop you can cultivate from early spring to early winter (though some varieties enjoy warmer weather). It takes spinach six to ten weeks before the leaves are ready for harvest.

Beets require a moist environment to grow well. Hence, it is necessary to water them regularly. Beetroot prefers full sun but will tolerate partial shade in a warmer climate. It's widely believed that beetroot is mainly a winter or mild weather crop, but they are relatively hardy and will grow in cooler to warm conditions (not freezing, but not scorching either, right in the middle of two extremes). Because of this, you can sow beetroot at the same time as spinach, though it does take beets slightly longer to grow than spinach (between seven and twelve weeks).

Other than that, both spinach and beets are low-maintenance crops that won't require much more than an occasional checkup from you to make sure the soil is moist but not wet and to see if they're ready to be harvested.

Harvesting

The best thing about harvesting spinach is that if you do it right, you can harvest it again from the same plant in less than a week. That's right! Spinach will regrow its leaves and do so relatively quickly, too. Once your spinach looks lush and ready, only harvest the outer leaves off all your plants instead of pulling out the entire plant roots. You can repeat this until the plant starts flowering or dies off at the end of the season.

Unfortunately, the same can't be said for beets since the plant can't regrow or do much without the root itself. Nevertheless, you can harvest beets as early as seven weeks after sowing. At this point, they will be roughly the size of golf balls (baby beets), or at around twelve weeks, they'll be the size of tennis balls. Keep them in the ground for a short time, as they only get less desirable as time goes on, and they might crack and start to rot. Do not discard the leaves and stems of beet plants, as they contain a significant amount of nutrients. You can consume them, incorporate them into the soil, or use them as mulch or compost until the next planting season (ensure sufficient time to decompose).

If planning an entire guild sounds too overwhelming, start with two crops that do well together and scale up as you gain knowledge, experience, and confidence in your green thumbs. If you can't run, walk; if you can't walk, crawl. Please start somewhere, though. Once again, it all comes down to your short-term goals and using them as stepping stones to get you to where you want to be.

Companion Planting for an Increase in New Gardens

"The garden is a love song, a duet between a human being and Mother Nature."

— JEFF COX

A study by OnePoll found that 55% of non-gardening respondents wished they knew how to garden, and a large proportion of them were worried about their lack of knowledge. There is a huge number of people who put off their dream of nurturing a thriving garden because they think it's too much work or they don't have the necessary skills – but as you're seeing now, it's possible to build a self-sustaining garden that's easy to maintain with no experience at all.

If I look at all the gardening information available out there, I can see why people give up before they've even gotten started. It's overwhelming, and for many people, it's impossible to see how to actually get their garden off the ground – or even think about applying any of the information they come across.

This guide is designed to do something different. By focusing on companion planting, a method in which the garden does a lot of the work for itself, I aim to make gardening more accessible and empower those who might otherwise be discouraged to pick up their trowels and give it a go. And this is where I'd like to ask for your help as a beginner gardener. You can show other people that it's not as difficult as they fear and point them in the direction of their launch pad.

By leaving a review of this book on Amazon, you'll show people looking for an easy and effective route into gardening exactly

where they can find it – and you'll inspire them too.

Thank you so much for your support. A garden is a great source of joy, and I want everyone who dreams of building one to have the best chance of success. Together, we can help more gardens spring up everywhere.

Scan the QR code below to leave a review:

5

COMPANION PLANTING — HERBS

Herbs are the gift that keeps giving, from adding flavor or garnish to a dish to supplementing your medicine cabinet. And I'm not just talking about home remedies or teas here. The USDA reports that herbs, including essential prescription drugs, comprise roughly 40% of all medications sold in pharmacies. A lot of painkillers, anti-inflammatories, anesthetics, analgesics, sedatives, and even antidepressants are on the list of plant-derived medicines.

Granted, a lot of these chemicals are now synthetically made in labs (to make them more stabilized, concentrated, and mass-producible), but it doesn't change the fact that we got the ideas for most medicines we have today from plants that our ancestors used for thousands of years.

CLASSIC HERB PAIRINGS

Whether you're growing herbs for their health benefits or to spice up your cooking (or both), they also provide many advantages for your garden, namely pest management and disease prevention. You can interplant these herb pairings around your garden; make sure there are no conflicts of interest, so to speak (ensure the herbs are companions with the other fruits, vegetables, and flowers first).

Rosemary and Sage

If you've never cooked with rosemary, use it sparingly since you're a pinch away from turning a dish from elevated into overpowered. But beyond that, it also has beautiful foliage, and despite its strong scent, it goes well with many dishes.

Depending on how spiritual you are, you may or may not subscribe to the idea that sage can cleanse your home of evil spirits and even bring luck. Nevertheless, it adds much more than that to the table (or garden). These two herbs together result in a power couple specializing in keeping pests at arm's length.

Benefits

Due to the aromatic nature of rosemary and the fact that it's a flowering herb, it can ward off certain pests and attract pollinators. As a bonus, it leaves your garden smelling amazing. Rosemary is an easy herb to cultivate because it's drought-resistant and tolerates extreme hot and cold conditions very well.

Rosemary also has some exciting health benefits and is said to be anti-inflammatory, antimicrobial, and exhibit neuroprotective properties. This claim is evident from studies on the clinical effects of rosemary that show it can positively affect mood, learning, and memory, reduce pain and anxiety, and improve sleep (Rahbardar & Hosseinzadeh, 2020).

Sage also attracts pollinators, and they tend to flower for quite a while (can be evergreen in the right conditions), adding a layer of beautification to your landscape. Because it is excellent at accumulating nutrients (specifically potassium and calcium), you can compost it or even make "tea" out of it and add it back into your garden to nourish or replenish the soil for your fruiting crops.

Care and Maintenance

Rosemary, while being drought resistant, actually prefers the soil on the dryer side, just like sage. And both sage and rosemary do best in full sun. You can get away with watering this pairing once every two weeks or so. They will likely survive minimal watering but won't do well when overwatered.

But even though sage and rosemary have a lot in common regarding their sun and water requirements, they won't compete for the same nutrients—which makes them such great companions.

Sow rosemary seeds in late spring or when any threat of frost has passed (even though they're hardy, they're not indestructible; it's always better to be safe than sorry). It's important to note that, when sowing rosemary seeds, you should sprinkle a very light layer of soil over the seeds instead of burying them entirely because the seeds need to be exposed to sunlight to germinate. Rosemary is a light feeder, so planting them in soil with mixed compost will hold them over for quite some time; you only have to supplement with more compost once a year.

Sage seeds germinate slowly (can take up to a month), so it's best to propagate them indoors or buy seedlings from a nursery if you're impatient. Sage can be propagated from cuttings as well. You can also sow sage seeds directly into the soil at the same time as rosemary seeds, but remember they will take longer to pop up.

Both sage and rosemary are perennials, so they will be dormant (appear dead) in winter and reanimate in spring. To keep these hardy plants looking neat, trim them right before winter by cutting off dead leaves or flowers and about a third of the plant. Feel free to dry the healthy herb foliage you prune away and use them for tea or cooking.

Harvesting

A general rule of thumb for harvesting herbs is to snip off as much as you need but only take up to 20% of the plant at a time. This precaution ensures enough to retake it in a week or two while allowing new growth to catch up.

With rosemary, you always want to harvest the new growth. Avoid harvesting or cutting woody stems since this will alter the shape and spread of the rosemary bush but won't promptly encourage further growth. You'll be able to recognize new growth on your rosemary plant because the stems will still be tender and might be more saturated in color.

In the case of sage, you can take the same route: cut what you need. However, it can take a while before your sage plant is ready to be harvested. It is advisable to wait at least a year until the plant is fully grown and established before harvesting any leaves or giving it a trim.

Basil and Chamomile

Whether making your pesto sauce or trying to make a serving bowl full of jasmine rice look more sophisticated when hosting a family dinner, basil has got you covered. It's incredibly versatile and can be used fresh or dried.

Chamomile is best known for its calming properties, but it can also alleviate common cold symptoms, settle an upset stomach, and lower your risk for heart disease and cancer (Gupta, 2010). If that's not a reason to add it to your garden, what is?

Benefits

Did you know many home gardeners spray chamomile tea on their seedlings to prevent common crop ailments like "damping off," mildew, blight, and other fungal and bacterial infections? That's because chamomile has anti-bacterial and anti-fungal properties. The good news is that you can reap these benefits by planting chamomile in your garden.

Chamomile is also said to increase the amount of oil that basil produces, enhancing the taste and scent (also making basil more effective in pest management).

Care and Maintenance

Since we already covered the care and maintenance of basil in the previous chapter, we'll now focus on chamomile. Chamomile is a flowering herb that resembles dainty daisies that grow in clusters. They grow rather quickly, reaching maturity in as little as ten weeks. Chamomile is technically an annual herb, but it reseeds very well, and you might find it reappearing in your garden every year regardless.

Chamomile prefer full sun, but if you're growing them in a hotter climate, they might benefit from partial shade (preferably on scorching afternoons). Because they are annuals, chamomile will require rich, fertile soil for best results. Water the seedlings often until maturity, then reduce and allow the soil to dry slightly between watering them (timing may vary based on your climate).

Chamomile is quite a light feeder despite it being an annual and will thrive even in poor soil. However, you should still feed the soil with compost every few months for the basil's sake.

Harvesting

It's typically the chamomile flowers used for teas or cooking since leaves and stems tend to be bitter (though they are edible none-theless). It's safe to assume that everyone knows how to pick flowers, but to get the best flavor from your chamomile and encourage the plant to grow new ones, there are a few things to consider.

You want to harvest the chamomile flowers when fully open and fresh (not wilted or withered). Chamomile flowers will be ready for harvest once the plant is mature (roughly ten weeks). When you harvest chamomile, be sure to only pick the flowers by holding on to the stem with one hand and picking the flower with the other; this will encourage the plant to grow more flowers immediately.

Thyme and Oregano

Like most herb pairings in this chapter, the synergy of thyme and oregano goes beyond what they offer you in the kitchen. Thyme is rich in vitamins A and C, which can help maintain healthy skin, mucus membranes, and vision. It can also strengthen your immune system, reduce inflammation, and protect against certain infectious diseases.

Both oregano and thyme are distant relatives in the mint family tree, so while they are beautiful when in bloom and fantastic to cook with, you should treat them the same way you would mint (as aggressively invasive if you give it a chance), which is why I would advise growing this companion pairing in containers or pots instead of directly in your garden.

You might be asking yourself: "If oregano and thyme are cousins, wouldn't that make them rivalries in the garden?" That's just the thing! They're both perennials and light feeders so they will be fine together in decently fertile soil (with yearly compost top-ups).

Benefits

Thyme and oregano offer your garden many benefits, especially if they're moveable (planted in pots). Relocating this pairing will allow you to place them where needed intermittently and move them indoors during the winter. These herbs are drought and frost-tolerant but don't like wet soil.

Thyme and oregano are flowering herbs that attract beneficial insects and pollinators while repelling garden pests with their scent.

Care and Maintenance

The most significant selling point of this pairing is its low mainte-nance needs. The hardest part is honestly keeping an eye on it to ensure it doesn't take over your garden (which is a problem easily fixable by simply planting them in pots or containers). Remember that nutrient-dense soil may be bad for both thyme and oregano; an initial compost or aged manure treatment to give the seedlings a good start to grow big and strong will suffice for a long time.

The mint family are the weeds of the herb world; they multiply and end up everywhere if you're not careful. For this reason, you'll need to check on them occasionally when cultivating them directly in your garden and remove any unwanted seedlings that might have popped up.

Thyme and oregano require full sun and weekly watering (make sure the soil has dried out somewhat in between watering). Mulch is always a good idea, but because thyme and oregano dislike overly moist soil, your best option is tree bark, a long-lasting mulch that you must only replace once a year. Besides that, you'll have to trim them back every so often to keep things neat and to encourage new growth.

Harvesting

Because thyme and oregano are such hardy plants, you can't go wrong with how or even how much you harvest (as long as you're not stripping them from all their leaves entirely or cutting them off at the base).

To harvest thyme or oregano, cut or pick off an inch of stem, with leaves attached from the tip of the various branches (which will be the newest growth available and taste the best). When dried, the flavor profile of thyme and oregano will change entirely to what they taste when fresh.

Cilantro and Dill

There's some debate about whether it's called cilantro or coriander. Most people believe it depends on where you live, and while there is some truth, there's a legitimate distinction between them. So, let's settle this once and for all: cilantro and coriander come from the same plant. When referring to the leaves and stems, it's cilantro. Coriander refers specifically to the seeds that cilantro plants produce.

While both come from the same plant, cilantro and coriander are technically not interchangeable terms because they refer to two separate things. Cilantro, as in the leaves and stems of the cilantro plant, has an entirely different taste and flavor than the seeds (coriander). You can't substitute cilantro for coriander in a recipe.

Cilantro, or coriander, is the oldest herb that we know of in the world. It dates back at least 5,000 years! It can also lower your cholesterol levels.

Dill doesn't have as much drama or controversy surrounding its name, but it does like to hang out with cilantro. Most people believe that dill flowers are edible and soothe the digestive system, just like most other flowering herbs.

Benefits

Planting cilantro and dill together really compounds their pest-repellent abilities. Dill is known to keep aphids and spider mites away, while cilantro chases flies, moths, and other fruit-boring pests. Mosquitoes are also not too fond of the smell of cilantro, which means fewer bites for you when working in the garden.

When planting this herb pair in pots, you can place them near your other guilds, specifically next to your leafy vegetables (spinach, lettuce, kale, etc.) and onions. Some say thyme improves the flavor of potatoes and onions, though, as we mentioned, this is purely opinion-based as of now and not scientifically verifiable.

If you're up for extra maintenance and want to cultivate this guild pairing directly in your garden bed, they will protect your soil from erosion and offer some ground cover with their foliage.

Care and Maintenance

Cilantro and dill seedlings will require regular watering, but they need substantially less water once they mature. However, if you wait too long between watering sessions, the plants may flower earlier, which could be an issue since it's always best to harvest herbs before they flower.

Both cilantro and dill are annual herbs, which means they grow quickly and only produce leaves for a handful of weeks before they start flowering. The good news is they are very efficient at reseeding themselves, meaning you might not even need to plant them again the following year; they'll appear.

The maintenance requirements of this pairing are minimal. Their root systems are shallow, and as long as you space them at least six inches apart, they will thrive together without trying to outcompete each other for nutrients. The soil should be well-draining and somewhat fertile. Whether you're growing them in pots or your garden bed, they prefer full sun but will tolerate partial shade.

Harvesting

Cilantro will be ready for its first harvest in 30 days, but if it's coriander you're after, you'll need to wait for it to flower and produce seeds (around three months after sowing or propagation). To harvest cilantro, go for the tender, new leaves at the very tip of the branches. To harvest coriander, wait for the flowers to wither and turn brown before snipping them off and breaking open the flower head. Separate the seeds from the plant debris and store them. You can use a pestle and mortar or put them in a pepper grinder to make your life easier when using them as seasoning.

To harvest dill (which you can do in approximately 70 days after sowing), you can snip off the top few inches of a branch or two to use. You can also harvest the edible flowers or seeds for cooking purposes, though you'll have to wait for the dill to flower or produce seeds first.

Parsley and Chives

Regarding the versatility and popularity of herbs, parsley will easily breach the top five in such a list (or it should, at least). Parsley and chives are widely used in or on a dish. Nothing says "I have my life together," like topping a dish you made from scratch with chives or parsley that you grew yourself.

Parsley has a distinct flavor profile, but it's more subtle and won't easily overpower a dish (like rosemary would, for instance). And that's why it's a staple in many homes and gardens. Not only is it easy to grow and beneficial for your garden, but it's also subtle yet noticeable. Iconic!

Chives are smaller, thinner, and more delicate versions of an onion. They're not onions, but they are related to one another. The mild onion flavor of chives can quickly go lost during even a short cooking period (plus, they wilt as soon as they hit the pan, which doesn't make for a very appealing sight), which is why they're predominantly a garnish. Nevertheless, they also have all the gardening benefits of onions.

Benefits

Is there anything parsley can't do? For starters, it's rich in vitamin C, aids in oral health (for you and your pets), it's a natural diuretic (which can help remove acid build-up, alleviating pain and other symptoms related to gout and arthritis), relieves indigestion, can be used in skincare, and can be used as a natural de-wormer for dogs and cats.

Furthermore, you'll be able to spot a nutrition imbalance or iron deficiency in your soil from the color of the parsley plant's leaves (if they turn yellow, you'll know it's time to add compost or aged manure to the soil). You can also use parsley as a trap crop for any vegetable or fruit guild since it attracts aphids and predatory insects (that might keep them in check, so they don't kill the parsley plant).

Besides making sour cream and chives dip for chips or baked potatoes, chives have much more to offer. You can use them as living mulch or ground cover crops, attract pollinators, and deter the same pests that other members of the allium family do. Chives can be "chopped and dropped" (used as fertilizer by simply picking the leaves and sprinkling them around the base of nearby crops right then and there).

Care and Maintenance

Parsley requires full sun (at least six hours) and fertile soil, so prepare your garden or pot soil with the appropriate nutrition. Parsley roots are on the shallow side but are considered tap roots, so make sure your soil can accompany an underground growing space of at least 12 inches deep (for a mature parsley plant).

Remember that parsley is a biennial, which means you'll be able to enjoy and harvest fresh parsley for two years. However, if you leave it to flower and drop seeds, parsley will reseed. Parsley is easy to maintain and care for, but it can be challenging to grow from seed. Buying parsley seedlings from a nursery might be easier if you're a beginner gardener.

Chives, on the other hand, are easy to grow from seeds. They're hardy perennials and will keep growing back yearly and throughout the growing season if you harvest them correctly. The only care and maintenance you need to dish out is dividing or breaking up (and replanting) dense patches every couple of years and ensuring the soil has plenty of nitrogen.

Sow or propagate your chive seeds a few weeks before expecting the last spring frost. Chive sprouts are delicate, so allow them to grow for at least eight weeks in a seedling tray, and be careful when transplanting if you go that route. Nevertheless, they are frost-tolerant and will regrow through the snow the following year.

Harvesting

It's always advisable to wait until a plant is mature before you harvest any leaves. A good rule of thumb for parsley is to wait until the plant has three leaf segments (or branches) before taking some. Harvest parsley from the outer edges of the plant first to give the very young and tender leaves in the middle time to mature a bit longer.

Chives grow in clusters of what looks like grass and are known to withstand heavy harvests. You can harvest every single chive, and as long as you leave the roots intact and about two to three inches from the base of the plant, it will regrow within a couple of weeks. The only reason I don't advise harvesting all your chives at once is so you can gather them again once you need them and not have to wait.

You can plant several guilds together in the same garden bed based on your gardening goals and planned guilds (or pairings). You'll need to ensure they get along, but this strategy will help you reap the most benefits from companion planting.

Herbs are the perfect place to start if you need to be more confident in your gardening skills. Most are hardy, easy to grow and maintain, and will bring life to your garden in preparation for more guilds or pairs!

6

COMPANION PLANTING — FRUITS

L et's not kid ourselves; fresh produce has become ridiculously expensive. And who doesn't like a flavorful, seasonal fruit salad? You can kill two birds with one stone by growing and serving your fruit salad without entering a grocery store.

Besides epic bragging rights, you can also whip up fresh smoothies in the morning, make jams or conserves, or pluck a few snacks while tending the garden. Do you know what they say about an apple a day? It's the best thing since sliced bread. No, wait, that's not it.

CLASSIC FRUIT PAIRINGS

However, if you want to spin it, a garden filled with fruits will benefit you so much that it's hard to argue against having one. In this chapter, we'll review the best companion planting pairs suited for small gardens (but you can certainly scale up if you have the space to do so).

Strawberries and Borage

We know and love them; please give it up for Strawberries! Interestingly, strawberries aren't berries; they are technically not even considered fruit (since their seeds are on the outside instead of the inside). Tiny fruits embed each strawberry seed, resulting in the visible seeds on the outside. So, a strawberry is a collection of small fruits joined together. It's okay; we forgive you for lying to us, strawberries.

Strawberries are easily one of the easiest fruits to grow yourself, even from seed. However, they are prone to many pests that enjoy these juicy, sweet, non-berries, which is where borage comes in. Besides having one of the more unique flowers, borage comes in peace and will help your strawberries thrive.

Benefits

Borage is an excellent choice for pairing with your strawberries. The deep purple flowers of borage look phenomenal next to the bright red fruits. In addition to this, the mature foliage of borage is thick and hairy (snails, slugs, and worms don't like this). By planting borage around your strawberries, you can ward off pests, attract beneficial insects that feed on any remaining strawberry-loving pests, and bring pollinators to your midst so your strawberry bushes will produce a bigger and better yield.

Allegedly, borage also improves the taste of strawberries, though this is just an old gardener's tale, so you should take it with a grain of salt. This idea probably came from the fact that borage has a taproot that mines trace minerals and brings it closer to the soil surface for the strawberries to use, which (allegedly) makes the strawberries taste sweeter. But I'll let you be the judge of that.

Borage can protect your strawberries from (or improve their resistance to) diseases like fruit rot and wilt. But borage isn't just aesthetically pleasing; their flowers and young leaves are edible (they taste like slightly spicy cucumber) and a great addition to fruit salads.

What do strawberries do for the garden, you ask? Besides being delicious, they spread and cover the soil, suppressing weeds and keeping the soil aerated and moist on sunny days. You can plant strawberries in any open spot you have in the garden as living mulch or use trimmed foliage as actual mulch.

Care and Maintenance

Borage is an annual, which is a shame, but it also means they're easy to grow and maintain. The low maintenance makes up for the fact that you'll have to replant them yearly. Similar to strawberries, they're great gap fillers for any bare spots you may have. Borage can grow to be quite large, though, so make sure there's at least a diameter of 18 inches available for it.

You can sow borage seeds directly into your garden bed in mid-spring; they don't like to be transplanted. Borage will thrive in the soil even without compost preparation; if you ensure the soil is well-draining and has at least partial sun (4-6 hours), you can set it and forget it. Borage will reseed by itself if you let it. All you need to do is let a couple of flowers stay on the plant until it dies in winter. Just remember to thin out the herd in mid-spring so you don't end up with more than you need or more than your garden can handle.

Even though borage doesn't require fertile soil, strawberries very much do. So, staying on top of your strawberries' dietary requirements would be best by topping the soil with compost every month and every other week once they flower. Like most fruiting plants, strawberries need full sun (at least eight hours for strawberries) to produce fruits.

Strawberries are perennials, but they will send out what's called "runners" from time to time, from which an entirely new strawberry plant will grow. This process is essentially an asexual form of procreation. Having too many strawberry plants is not impossible, but you should keep an eye on this and occasionally thin out any new sprouts (or cut-off runners).

Harvesting

The harvesting process for both strawberries and borage is straightforward, almost self-explanatory. As mentioned, if you are harvesting borage for consumption, only harvest young, tender leaves that have yet to thicken or develop hairs. The thick, hairy borage leaves aren't harmful but have an unpleasant feel in the mouth and can be pretty tough. Harvesting the flowers before they seed and when they are open, vibrant, and healthy-looking would be best. If they're wilting or turning brown, they're no good. Pick the flowers or leaves you require and make a pretty salad.

Strawberries are ready for harvesting when they are entirely red. However, if you have a different variety of strawberries, the berries' time to ripen or mature will vary. In the case of the standard red strawberry, it will take about four to six weeks after the flowers open before you can start harvesting them. To do so, gently pick or snip the strawberry off the branch so you don't harm the plant.

The best strategy is to harvest strawberries every three days and only pick the ripest ones, entirely red and plump, while leaving some smaller or paler ones on the plant to continue ripening.

Strawberries don't store well (even in the fridge), so harvesting every few days will ensure you have only the freshest strawberries all season.

Apple Trees and Comfrey

Have you ever wondered how bonsai trees work? Are they genetically modified? Are they bred explicitly over thousands of years? And why am I bringing this up? Here's a fun fact about trees: The root ball's size determines the tree's size. The word "bonsai" means "planted in a container". And regardless of the size of the tree, it will still grow fruits and produce seeds. So yes, you can successfully grow an apple tree (or any other tree for that matter) in a large container, and it will grow to fit the size of the container perfectly and not an inch more (unless you size up the pot).

However, while trees planted in containers will be a smaller version of the regular-sized tree, the fruits will be regular-sized. If you have the space to grow a full-sized apple tree, do that. But if you're growing it in a large pot or container (I recommend the most significant container you can get your hands on), your best choice is self-fertile, dwarf apple tree varieties such as crab apples.

Comfrey is a member of the borage family and produces clusters of either purple, blue, yellow, or white flowers, depending on the variety you get. Together with apples, they benefit each other in many ways.

Benefits

Comfrey provides many of the same benefits as borage, like pest deterrence, attracting pollinators, weed management, and cycling nutrients. In addition, borage also acts as living mulch for your apple tree, protecting and shading the ground from erosion or excessive moisture loss. Comfrey also acts as a trap crop for apple maggot flies.

The benefits of having an apple tree are in its longevity. A single self-fertile apple tree will produce apples for many years to come. Established apple trees are hardy and resilient. You can use apple peels and cores to fertilize your garden by composting them or making fertilizer tea. Not to mention, they are easy to cultivate, care for, and maintain.

Care and Maintenance

Comfrey is a perennial crop found along riverbanks and grass-lands, so it's no surprise that it prefers soil that's always moist and at least partial shade (minimum of three hours a day). Like borage, mature comfrey leaves have a hairy texture. One of the major selling points is that it can be planted or grown at any time of the year if the soil is fresh.

Although comfrey has a history of being classed as edible, that's no longer the case since it contains pyrrolizidine alkaloids, which can cause liver damage in humans and pets when ingested. So, it might be best to stick to growing the flower for its beauty and other benefits rather than for consumption. You can, however, substitute comfrey for borage if you want a more functional crop.

Once established, comfrey requires yearly nitrogen top-ups in compost or aged manure sprinkled over the top layer of soil. It's also not partial on soil types and will grow in clay, sandy, or loamy soil. Given that you're pairing comfrey with an apple tree, you should opt for loamy, well-draining, fertile soil. If you give it what it needs while young, it will thank you by basically maintaining itself when it's mature.

Apple trees need full sun, well-draining and fertile soil, and regular irrigation (especially when fruiting) to yield the best. Choose a self-fertile variety if you only have space for one apple tree.

Prepare the garden bed or potting soil with a generous amount of compost. You can propagate seeds indoors or buy a young tree from a nursery and transplant it when ready. You can transplant a young apple tree at any time except when they're flowering or fruiting since this might negatively affect the yield, or you might lose the yield completely (winter is generally a safe bet when transplanting fruit trees of any kind).

Mulch your young apple tree and wait for it to become established enough (at least a year) before planting comfrey, borage, or anything else alongside it. Quick-growing crops might smother and kill a young fruit tree.

Your apple tree will need its first haircut when it's in its third year of growth and then as needed (inspect the tree at the beginning of every spring when it is still dormant; this makes it easier to see what needs attention). You can remove dead, damaged, or diseased leaves and branches at any time without risking the well-being of the tree in question; in fact, it will always benefit the tree if you do this. However, slightly pruning a tree differs from stripping dead branches and foliage.

Only prune your fruit tree when it's dormant (in winter or early spring). Only cut the central leader (the middle, main stem that goes into the soil and tapers towards the top of the tree) once the tree is fully mature or after its third year of growth. During the tree's first year of growth, you want to ensure that the branches grow evenly from the central leader. If two branches are too close together, cut one of them off.

In the second year, you want to remove competing leaders (scaffolding branches growing too vigorously and affecting the tree's shape). In the third year, trim the branches coming out of the central leader into a pyramid shape (so the bottom branches are long and get shorter as you reach the top of the tree).

You'll have to inspect your tree yearly and trim off any branches attempting to grow too low (underneath the canopy or near the base of the tree), branches that look like they're growing vertically upwards or downwards from a scaffolding branch, and any branches that look like they're emerging in clumps. If branches are rubbing against each other, remove the newest or thinnest one by cutting it close to whichever branch it's originating from.

You also want to reduce all scaffolding (or lateral) branches by a third of their length. This reduction will encourage the remaining branches to grow thicker so your tree can support more weight (resulting in a more significant yield).

Lastly, it would help if you netted your apples to protect them from birds. You can use bird (or pigeon) nets or pest netting as soon as baby apples form, but mosquito nets or any mesh fabric will also work. Secure the netting around the fruit with a ribbon or twine (most pest nets will have drawstrings) until they're ready for harvesting.

Harvesting

Your apples will be ready to harvest when they are the proper color (variety dependent) and come off the tree with a gentle twist and tug. You can have a taste right then and there to determine whether they're ready for harvesting. Standard apple trees will only start bearing fruits five to ten years after planting; if you're impatient, go for dwarf varieties that will bear fruit in two to three years.

Nevertheless, apples will generally be ready for harvesting at around 115 to 135 days after 90% of the flowers on the tree have opened (also known as full bloom).

Blueberries and Rhododendrons

Rhododendrons are azaleas because they are too closely related to class them as separate plant varieties (according to botanists). Someone else calls the shots because we call them two different things here. The flowers look slightly different, but both are beautiful, nonetheless.

Blueberries are notoriously difficult to form a companion guild with because they prefer acidic soil, whereas 99% of common garden crops don't. But rhododendrons share this love for soil with a pH of below six at the very least. In the spirit of diversity, we can't let our blueberry brethren stand alone!

Benefits

Blueberries are a sustainable crop because they are pest and disease-resistant (I'm guessing most insects and microorganisms also don't do too well in acidic soil). To be clear, this doesn't mean you won't ever have a pest problem in your blueberry bushes, so you should still monitor your crops and take some precautionary steps. You can use neem oil to make a solution to spray on the blueberry bush to protect against pests like aphids.

There are also a lot of blueberry varieties that are self-fertile if you don't have the space to grow more than one bush. Blueberries are a "superfood" because they have many health benefits, and it's hard to list them all without people thinking you're a sales rep.

Both blueberries and rhododendrons attract pollinators, so there's that. But, honestly, that's as far as their mutual relationship goes. They both have shallow roots and can be grown in smaller pots.

This pairing will be most beneficial if your garden has acidic soil that you want to use effectively. Growing something is better than nothing, and beggars can't be choosers. Of course, if you love blueberries and want to develop them, don't let anything stop you. They're easy to grow and maintain in proper conditions.

Care and Maintenance

The most important step to cultivating this guild is preparing your soil. Blueberries prefer soil with a pH level between four and five and should also be well-draining and fertile with lots of organic matter. Gardening stores sell acidic soil, but make sure it's organic. Alternatively, you can make the soil acidic by adding fertilizers that contain high levels of ammonium, nitrate, urea, phosphor, and sulfur.

However, you will need some way of testing the soil's pH levels. In this case, a reusable pH testing machine is a good investment. After you've amended the soil, give it a few months and test the soil again. Repeat the process until the soil reaches the preferred pH levels and test again every few months afterward. The soil pH levels will try to correct themselves and slowly move to a neutral state (especially if you're making previously neutral soil acidic). You must amend the soil again to maintain the preferred acidity levels. This maintenance is the bulk of the work when growing blueberries.

Blueberries grow well in full sun (but will tolerate minimal shade), like cold winters, and don't compete well with weeds, so make sure you mulch them generously. Mulching with pine needles and sawdust can help keep the soil acidic for longer. Blueberries should be watered deeply once a week, with the soil soaked for the first few inches. An irrigation system will save you some trouble, but it's not a requirement.

It would be best to space blueberry bushes at least 4 feet apart. If your blueberry bush's leaves start to yellow, it's a sign the pH is not low enough. To fix this, add garden sulfur or aluminum sulfur to the topsoil and water the soil to help it settle before mulching the area.

Harvesting

Blueberries are perennials, and while they can start producing berries in their second or third growing year, the quality and quantity of production will reach their full potential once the plant is at least six years old. Remember to pinch off any flower buds on the blueberry bush in their first and second year to encourage its general growth first; this will result in a bigger and better third-year harvest since the plant will be more established than it would have been if you didn't remove flower buds in the first two growing years.

How do you know when blueberries are ripe? The easiest and most reliable way is to pick a few and give them a taste. But as a general guideline, ripe blueberries are a deep blue-purple with a light gray dusting of what looks like powder and will be plump (but not firm) to the touch. A very firm blueberry with a hint of red (or that's still white or green) is not ready yet and will be tart and unpleasant to eat. Blueberries won't ripen further once picked like tomatoes or peppers, so only harvest them if you're confident they're ripe.

The trick to harvesting the sweetest blueberries is leaving them on the bush for at least a week *after* they've turned that deep blue-purple color completely. The berries will come off the branch effortlessly; hold a bucket or basket under a cluster of blueberries and pick them off with your free hand. You might have to pick out some stems and leaves afterward. Store them in the fridge unwashed (they'll stay fresh for up to a week refrigerated), and only wash them before eating or using them. The moisture might make them spoil sooner if you prewash them.

Your rhododendrons will unfortunately not bear fruit, but at least they're pretty to look at. Prune away dead, damaged, or diseased foliage or flowers as needed so it stays looking pretty and productive.

Grape and Lavender

Most bunching grape varieties are self-fertile, so you only need one grapevine to produce a yield, which is excellent news when you're short on space. Grapes can also start bearing fruit from as early as their second year. That's alright, considering they're perennials that will likely outlive you (most grapevine varieties can live to 100 years old!).

Then, of course, there's lavender, another distant relative of the flowering mint family. Its everyday use is for its calming properties in the form of essential oils, skincare or bath products, and even tea. Additionally, it can alleviate other health qualms and symptoms like migraines, anxiety, inflammation, allergies, and insomnia, to name just a few. Lavender is a big deal in the world of aromatherapy. Place a bouquet of freshly picked lavender in your bathroom and experience a relaxing bath.

However, lavender is also used in the kitchen and can be dried, finely chopped, and used (or infused) in rubs, marinades, sauces, desserts, syrups, sorbets, ice cream, and more. It can also be used whole, fresh, or dried as a decorative garnish. Nevertheless, lavender is an excellent addition to your garden and holds a lot of tricks up its purple sleeves.

Benefits

Homemade wine, anyone? I'm not here to judge what you do with the grapes once you've grown and harvested them. But growing lavender with your grapes is a good idea. While fruiting crops don't generally bring a lot to the table in companion planting—since we mainly grow them for the benefit of eating them—grapes are more beneficial for your garden than you might've expected.

Beneficial insects love grapes, which provide built-in pest management. They are also significant producers in the right conditions; on average, a single, established, healthy grapevine can produce between eight and ten pounds of grapes annually. That's more than enough for a small family.

Even when your grapevines are not producing fruit, they add charisma and interest to any garden in any season. Let them engulf a garden archway, belvedere, or pergola, and see your garden of dreams come to life (and it's super functional, too). Now pair that vision with some lush lavender, and you'll be the go-to person for hosting get-togethers with friends and family.

But lavender is also not one to sit back and look pretty. It is naturally pest-resistant and repellent and will also draw pollinators to your garden, benefiting all your crops. Lavender (a hardy perennial) thrives in most climates, is easy to grow, and can withstand drought.

Care and Maintenance

Lavender and grapevine guilds require little maintenance if you set them up for success. Both lavender and grapes have a low need for fertilizer. Too much nitrogen can increase the risk of grapes getting fungal diseases, and too much water will reduce the grapevine roots' ability to absorb enough nutrients (and can lead to root rot). And lavender prefers drier soil anyway.

Grapes are typically grown from cuttings rather than seeds. You can buy a grapevine plant from a nursery or purchase grapevine cuttings online (ensure the website is reputable). To grow a grapevine from a cutting, prepare a nursing tray or container with well-draining, fertile soil. Cut one end of the branch so it's slanted, like how you would cut a ribbon to keep it from fraying. Then, stick the cutting into the soil with the sloping end pointing up. Water the soil well so it stays moist but not soggy; proper hydration at this point is critical for the cuttings to grow good roots.

After about two months, the roots will be long enough to survive, and you can transplant them into their final spot in the garden. Yes, you can plant them in containers, but the containers need to be a minimum size of 15 gallons. Avoid dark-colored pots or containers since this might cause the roots to overheat. Wood is a good option. Wouldn't it be ironic if you grew grapes in an old wine barrel? If you ever need this information, an octave cask would be about 15 gallons.

Leave your grapevine be for an entire year to allow the roots and vines to become established. Then, in the winter of its second year, cut it down to right above the first two buds (little protrusions or "pimples" on the trunk). A drastic pruning indeed, but two thicker branches will grow from those two buds you left. This pruning, however extreme it may seem, will ensure your grapevine is as strong as it needs to be to carry a more significant yield. The year after this will mainly be spent "training" the vine by wrapping and tying it to your trellis or support structure.

Speaking of which, your grapevine will need a sturdy, long-lasting trellis or support for climbing. Remember, grapevines will live for many years and develop thick, solid, heavy vines and grapes; if it breaks, you can't replace the trellis or support without putting the vine in grave danger; if you can, go for a thicker steel structure of sorts from the very start.

After the second year, your grapevine will be all set up and ready to produce. The only maintenance you need from here on out is yearly pruning. You'll want to cut away any runners that grow beyond or away from the trellis and any dead or damaged branches.

Grapes and lavender need full sun and will benefit from a light layer of mulch. If you plant lavender with your grapes, ensure that the grapes aren't overshadowing the lavender. Lavender is slow to germinate (it can take up to a month) but grows steadily and will bloom for the first time in its second year of growth.

Sow lavender seeds over prepped soil, but don't cover or push them into the soil; they need exposure to sunlight to germinate. Pruning lavender is optional, requiring only yearly pruning to keep the garden neat. Funnily enough, you can also grow lavender from cuttings.

Harvesting

Like blueberries, the simplest way to tell whether your grapes are ready to be harvested is to taste a few straight from the vine. The flowers on the grapevine will stick around for a couple of weeks before they turn into small "berries." Typically, grapes will be ripe enough to harvest three months after their small berry-like first appearance (usually in late summer to early fall).

To harvest your grapes, pick entire bunches by cutting the stems. Don't pick the grapes individually; besides this method being wildly inefficient and labor intensive, your grapes will last longer if you leave them (and store them) attached to the stems.

Lavender doesn't lose its fragrance when dried; it's one of its many fine qualities. You can harvest lavender when the flower buds open to get the best flavor and fragrance. Cut the lavender flower at the base of the stem or as long or short as you need it to be. Did you know that lavender flowers are edible and can add color and taste to salads? You can also make tea out of it. But be careful; use it sparingly as it's very fragrant.

Peach and Garlic

Did you know that the fuzz on peaches is there to protect them from pests and other environmental factors? If only all crops came with this helpful feature pre-installed.

A peach is a "stone" fruit, which is a fancy way to say it has a thin skin and contains a seed within a hard pit (or stone) in the middle of the fruit. Apricots, cherries, plums, nectarines, and the like are all stone fruits. The point is that these decadent fruits contain large amounts of vitamin C and antioxidants, making them a great companion for garlic.

Garlic bread, garlic butter, crushed, minced, or confit are some of its uses. Garlic is another kitchen staple in most households. I can't remember the last time I made a dish without it! Some side effects of consuming garlic may include Mosquitoes (and occasionally, people) giving you a wide berth, improved digestive function, and a delicious meal. As long as you have garlic, do you even need anything else?

Benefits

Garlic is to your garden as a knight is to a king. Garlic, like all alliums, has strong pest-repellent properties and will keep aphids, peach tree borers, weevils, and fruit flies far away. It also adds potassium back into the soil and has natural anti-fungal attributes, which will keep the soil fertile and the roots of your peach tree healthy. You can also use garlic as living mulch to suppress weeds or chop and drop once it's time to harvest. Nothing goes to waste here!

This example is another guild pairing you can effortlessly grow in a large container or raised garden bed. Peach trees and garlic are hardy crops, and low maintenance is a benefit.

While peach trees don't do as much for the garden as garlic does, they benefit us with their longevity and abundant yields. And they provide shelter for beneficial insects and pollinators. It's not much, but it's honest work.

Care and Maintenance

Growing a peach tree from a seed is possible but will take some finesse. This requirement is because a hard coating or pit surrounds the seed; you'll need to first stratify the seed (with the pit intact) in the fridge for four months, then you'll need to gently crack open the seed without damaging the embryo on the inside (a nutcracker works well). After this, keep the pit in a paper towel or a seedling starting tray and consistently moist. Creating a greenhouse effect by placing the seed wrapped in a damp paper towel in a Ziploc bag or covering the seedling tray with a clear plastic container will prevent it from drying out and increase humidity levels (which aids in germination and early growth).

You can transplant your seedling into a bigger pot or its final place in the garden (in late winter after the ground has thawed) once it has its first set of true leaves. But if you want to avoid all this, purchase a young peach tree (about one year old) from a nursery to transplant. Prepare the soil with a complete fertilizer and top up twice yearly for the first three years of growth and water every other week (or every week in hot summers).

In either event, the young peach tree will need some attention eventually. Once the tree is about a year old, prune the shoots off the top by two or three buds. If you purchased a young tree, you can do this immediately or at the end of the following winter. This pruning keeps the tree from growing too tall and encourages it first to send all resources to the main branches to form a strong structure.

In the second year, you want to clean up those branches that matured in the first year. You do this by cutting back any scaffolding branches and leaving only the three thickest branches stemming from the leader (the stem). Also, remove any shoots forming below these three main branches.

After this, you want to leave the tree alone and only prune away the three D's (dead, damaged, or diseased matter) every year. Peach trees generally start bearing fruit in their fourth year. Peach trees need full sun and prefer colder winters to produce the best fruit.

Plant garlic in the fall before the first frost or in early spring in warmer climates because garlic also requires a short stratification period. It's very tricky to grow garlic from seed, so I advise you to grow garlic from the garlic itself. That's right! You can plant individual garlic cloves directly into the ground, and it will grow into an entire garlic plant.

Garlic likes full sun and moist, fertile, well-draining soil. To plant garlic, start by preparing the soil with fertilizer. Separate the cloves from each other, leaving the papery layer surrounding each one intact. Only use the biggest cloves for planting and use the rest for cooking.

Plant your garlic cloves two to three inches deep and at least four inches apart. You'll notice that each clove has a pointy and rounded end; plant the garlic's sharp end facing up. Cover the holes and add a thick layer of straw mulch (which will retain moisture and suppress weeds that will steal nutrients away from your garlic). In about two months, you'll be able to see leaves emerge from the mulch.

Water garlic weekly for the first month, reduce frequency after this, and account for rainy weather. Garlic should receive about an inch of water once a week; excess water will cause the garlic to rot. It takes about nine months for the garlic to mature and be ready for harvest.

You can try growing garlic from store-bought ones, but if you do this, ensure that the garlic is organic. They will often spray garlic with chemicals that discourage sprouting for a longer shelf-life; buying organic garlic reduces the chances of it having had this treatment. Alternatively, you can buy a few garlic plants from a nursery and save some from those for future sowing.

Harvesting

Peaches are ready to be harvested when no sign of green is present on the fruit. The color gradient of the peach may differ depending on your variety, but generally, the bottom of the peach should be yellow and the top red or deep orange. The good news is that even if you pick a peach before it's fully ripened, it will continue to ripen off the tree (place it in a paper bag, which you should keep in a dark cupboard).

As long as you pick it when there's no green left, you can let them ripen after harvesting. Peaches are a summer fruit and will generally be ready for harvest during this time. Use a light hand when harvesting peaches because they bruise easily. They should come off the tree with a gentle twist; if they don't, you can use some pruners to cut the stems (but bear in mind that these might not be fully ripe yet).

Garlic is ready to be harvested when most leaves or foliage have turned yellow or brown. You can dig one up to check for size. Avoid pulling the garlic up by the leaves since they are usually dry when the garlic is mature and will break off easily. Instead, use a garden fork to lift the garlic out of the soil from underneath the bulb.

Brush off any soil from the garlic bulbs and allow them to dry out or "cure" for about a month in a cool, well-ventilated room (or in a shaded area outside) before use.

Make sure you have enough space to start a guild. There is always a way to grow some fresh produce in small gardens or outdoor spaces. If you've been living under the impression that you can't have fruit trees because your garden is too small, now is the time to get rid of that idea and grow whatever you want!

7

COMPANION PLANTING — FLOWERS

You give them to your significant other on Valentine's Day or your anniversary. You bring them to your friend in the hospital to make them feel better. You use them as a pop of color on the dinner table when it's your turn to host family events.

Flowers do a lot of things outside of the soil as well as inside. Sure, they're pretty but also necessary for a functional and healthy garden. And quite a lot of them are edible, too.

CLASSIC FLOWER PAIRINGS

Do you want a garden that's both edible and beautiful? Companion planting allows you to enjoy the benefits of multiple plant species, enhancing your yields and creating a more diverse and healthy garden. While most fruits and vegetable crops do spawn their flowers for reproduction, having additional flowering plants to draw in some beneficial wildlife (and helping save the bees while you're at it) is in the best interest of your garden.

Marigolds and Almost Anything

Remember when I told you that you can never go wrong with marigolds? That's because beans and cabbage are the only known "bad" companions for marigolds. Because they attract the same pests, technically speaking, you can use marigolds as a trap crop to protect your beans and cabbage. The only time you shouldn't pair marigolds with another crop is when their requirements differ entirely.

For example, marigolds will fare poorly with blueberries because marigolds need a higher soil pH level. Marigolds will fare poorly with crops that prefer shaded areas or dry soil. But the margin of crops needing shade and dry soil is slim.

Since we already covered marigolds in a previous chapter, I'll summarize their benefits, care, and maintenance requirements.

Benefits:

- Easy to grow.
- Flowers are edible.
- Pest and nematode management.
- They attract pollinators and predatory insects (additional pest control).
- Serve as a trap crop.
- Use as mulch (chop and drop).

Care and Maintenance:

- They require full sun.
- Prepare the soil with fertilizer or compost and top up yearly (before flowering and not during winter).

- Allow soil to dry out somewhat between each watering (water once a week).
- Avoid overhead watering (water at the base).
- Cut off spent flowers to promote new flowers to grow immediately.

Sunflowers and Cucumbers

Did you know you can eat sunflowers? No, not the seeds; I mean everything. You can harvest sunflower heads when the seed coatings haven't formed yet (or haven't hardened), pluck off the petals, slather some oil, and cook it on a grill. I haven't tried it yet, and I'm skeptical. But people say it tastes like corn on the cob, and artichoke had a baby out of wedlock.

Nevertheless, sunflowers and cucumbers make for great companion plants. Note: Grilling and eating whole sunflowers is not a requirement. But feel free to harvest the seeds for a future snack!

Benefits

Pairing your cucumbers with sunflowers is a great idea. The sturdy sunflower stalks are a natural trellis for the climbing cucumber vines, which saves valuable space in your garden. Sunflowers also attract pollinators and predatory insects, which are known to improve crop yield and manage certain pests and their offspring.

Sunflowers are hyper-accumulators and will absorb any heavy metals and toxic chemicals in the soil, making it generally healthier. Besides a natural trellis, pest control, pollinators, and healthier soil, you are left with beautiful flowers in your garden that you can harvest for decorations and snacks. The bright yellow leaves of sunflowers also compliment the cucumbers' greenery perfectly.

You can use cucumbers to benefit your garden in a few different ways. One of which is making liquid fertilizer. Cucumbers (specifically the skin and leaves) are high in vitamins and minerals, such as potassium and phosphorus, that aid in the health and growth of all plants. Save any cucumber skin you may have from peeling them, and place them in a container that has a lid. Fill the container with cucumber skins (or leaves) and water, secure the lid, and leave it to soak for at least five days.

After this, scoop out the cucumber skins (or leaves) and let them dry on parchment paper. Once the skins are dry, you can chop them into smaller pieces and sprinkle them onto the soil around any crops you may have, or you can burn them and use the ash in the same way for a quicker release of nutrients. In the meantime, you can use the cucumber water to water any crops that look like they could use a "pick me up" or dilute it and water your entire garden evenly.

Care and Maintenance

Sunflowers are not picky or high-maintenance crops at all. Give them water, any soil type, and full sun, and they will accomplish their goal of growing big and strong no matter what nature throws at them. Wait until the last frost has passed in spring and sow your seeds regularly in a sunny spot in well-draining, fertile soil and water for the first few weeks. Once your sunflowers mature, reduce watering to once a week. Sunflowers are drought-resistant, but the flowers *will* droop if the plant doesn't receive enough water.

Add slow-release compost or fertilizer to the soil for best results before planting. This way, you will only need to amend the soil the following year (sunflowers are annual, so you'll need to sow them again yearly). To prevent diseases like powdery mildew, root rot, rust, and wilt, ensure your sunflowers get enough air circulation and space them at least six inches from each other when planting to avoid overcrowding.

Cucumbers also require full sun and well-draining, fertile soil. Cucumbers are vining plants, so if you're planting the companion pair in a container, you may only be able to fit one cucumber plant with a couple of sunflowers (cucumbers need at least three feet between them).

Cucumbers' most crucial care instruction is regular watering and mulch because they need lots of moisture to develop and grow a plump yield. Not watering enough will lead to small, wrinkled, and even bitter cucumbers. When watering, water at the base since overhead watering or irrigation via sprinklers may cause the foliage and fruits to rot quickly. Refrain from overfertilizing the plant; stick to an initial round of fertilizer (before planting) and top the soil with liquid fertilizer approximately one week after blooms start appearing.

Plant sunflowers first and allow them to grow to about 12 inches tall before you sow the cucumber seeds. By the time your cucumbers start vining or even blooming, your sunflowers will be prominent and robust enough to provide enough structural support for your incoming cucumbers. Your cucumbers may need some trellis "training" to do this; wrap the vines and tendrils around the sunflowers as they grow (you can also use twine to secure them if necessary).

Harvesting

It would be best to harvest cucumbers when they're the right size and color according to the variation you're growing. Most cucumbers start yellow or pale and develop into a dark green as they mature and ripen. A ripened cucumber should be firm, have no soft or squishy spots, and no yellowing.

Once your cucumbers bloom and start forming small berry-like fruit, they will grow fast. Check on your cucumbers regularly and harvest them as soon as they are uniform in color, firm, and crisp. For pickling varieties, the ideal size is generally two inches long, while slicing varieties should be between six to ten inches long.

Cucumbers are best when not entirely ripe as seeds are hard and taste bitter, so selecting based on size is optimal. Because you're harvesting cucumbers before they are fully grown, they won't come off the vine as effortlessly as a ripe fruit would. Use gardening scissors or pruners to cut the cucumbers when harvesting to prevent damaging the plant (and affecting the growth of other cucumbers that aren't quite ready to be harvested yet).

Sunflower heads are ready to be harvested once the back of the flower is yellow. This colorization is when the seeds are fully formed and ready to be eaten. Because cucumbers and sunflowers are annuals, they will die together once the harvesting period is over. You can leave the roots in the ground over winter to feed the soil and allow the dead plant matter to stay on the ground as mulch to keep weeds from popping up. Simply till the decomposed leaves into the soil before planting again the following year.

Nasturtiums and Roses

I know what you're thinking: "But didn't you say gardening has to be functional?" I did say that, and I stand by that statement. But this guild pairing is more functional than you might think. Yes, both plants are flowers, and their primary function is beauty. However, nasturtiums (flowers, leaves, stems, and seeds) are edible and can add a fantastic peppery flavor to soups, stews, and garden salads.

Plus, if you interplant this pairing between all your other guilds, they are a valuable addition to your garden, not only in aesthetics.

Benefits

As mentioned, nasturtiums and roses beautify your garden, but you can also use them as trap crops for pests like aphids. But don't worry because they also attract hoverflies, ladybirds, and lacewings, which eat aphids and other common pests. So not only will you keep aphids away from your other crops, but the predatory insects will keep the aphid population in check.

While nasturtiums are an excellent living ground cover and chop and drop mulch, roses are drought-tolerant and don't require much maintenance to look (and smell) as beautiful as they do. Of course, all flowers (including roses and nasturtium) will bring pollinators to the garden, which is always a plus.

Care and Maintenance

Roses and nasturtiums both need full sun and well-draining, fertile soil. However, nasturtiums thrive and flower best in soil that's not overly fertilized, while roses need regular fertilizing for impressive blooms. For this reason, you should amend the soil lightly with fertilizer or compost before planting the pair and only "spot-fertilize" roses around the base with liquid fertilizer (but you can also use regular fertilizer as long as you're only feeding the roses).

Sow nasturtiums once the soil has warmed up enough (mid-spring is best). They rarely succumb to dehydration, so water them whenever you water the roses, which should be at least once a week (and water both at the base to avoid wetting the foliage). Nasturtiums only really need pruning if you want to neaten things up in the garden (in which case, be my guest).

Roses, on the other hand, will need minimal pruning. You should remove dead, damaged, and diseased matter throughout the year and as soon as you spot it. But other than that, cut back the previous year's growth to where the center of the branches (or canes) looks white. Remember: Major pruning should be done in late winter or early spring only, but you can remove brown branches, dead flowers, or leaves at any time.

Nasturtiums are annuals, but they tend to self-seed (meaning you probably won't need to replant them. Instead, you'll have to thin out the sprouts in spring), while roses are hardy perennials, which will become dormant in winter and come back to life in spring.

Harvesting

Nasturtium flowers and leaves taste peppery and can add color to a salad. Harvesting the flowers before they set seed would be best, so the best bet would be to pick them right as they open. The leaves taste best when young and crisp, so you should only harvest new growth.

To use nasturtium seeds as a caper substitute, pick them while they are still green and then pickle them in vinegar.

You'll likely harvest roses to display around the house, gift them to a friend, or sprinkle the leaves into your bubble bath. Regardless, for the best and longest-lasting result, harvest roses in mid-morning after the dew has dried, and only harvest roses that are still starting to open (cut the stem at a 45° angle). You can also dry the roses in salicylic acid for a longer-lasting, rustic display.

Petunias and Beans

There are so many crops you can pair up with beans, but if you want a better bean yield while adding a layer of pretty, beans and petunias are a good choice. This guild pair is especially great for beginner companion gardeners because it's so easy to take care of and can serve as that initial confidence boost you need to dive in even further!

Benefits

Petunias can act as a trap crop for bean beetles and aphids, but they also repel certain other pests and attract pollinators and predatory insects. This guild works in a very similar way to the previous guild pairing (nasturtiums and roses), but unlike nasturtiums, petunias aren't edible. But they are lovely and will have your garden buzzing with bees and butterflies!

Beans, being legumes, are perfect for soil health since they're nitrogen fixers. This characteristic means they increase nitrogen levels in the soil and make the nitrogen more accessible to nearby neighbors (in this case, your petunias). On top of this, beans are incredibly versatile in the kitchen and contain a lot of protein and fiber.

Care and Maintenance

Both beans and petunias have similar growing requirements: They need well-draining and fertile soil, regular watering (every couple of days when young and twice a week once established), and full sun. However, they will compete for nutrients if planted too close together. Sow beans and petunias at least a foot apart. For this reason, it might be wise to add a ground cover crop to the guild or mulch the garden bed (or container) well.

Petunias are biennials, meaning they complete their life cycle within two years before they die. But they are also known to self-seed quite effectively, and some might even make it through their third year, depending on which climate you're in. Most bean varieties are annual and will need planting again every year.

To cultivate climbing beans, you must offer support through a trellis. Remember to implement crop rotation unless you're planting in containers or raised garden beds (in which case you'll need a resting period every couple of years and amend the soil well between seasons).

Petunias and beans don't need pruning, but you might have to "train" your climbing beans so they utilize the support structure properly, and always remember to remove dead foliage.

As always, if you use certain plants as trap crops, you'll want to keep an eye on them to ensure pests are not overrunning them. Once a trap crop dies, nothing stops the still very much alive pests from looking elsewhere for sustenance and shelter. So, check on your petunias occasionally and cut off any stems or flowers with vast numbers of aphids or other pest babies (eggs) to help keep populations manageable.

Harvesting

You can harvest petunia flowers for display as you would any other flowers, but if you want them to reseed independently, leave a few flowers on the plant until they fall off by themselves so seeds can form, mature, and disperse via gravity.

Beans are a bit trickier. For starters, there are many different bean varieties, and the type of beans you grow will determine the best harvest time. But a general rule of thumb is to harvest bean pods before they harden and turn brown. Just for reference, bush beans will be ready for harvest about 50 days after flowering, and pole beans will be ready for harvest around 60 days after flowering.

The best advice I can give is to look up how your specific type of beans or pods should look and feel when they're ready to be harvested or how long it typically takes after flowering. Leaving them on the bean plant for too long will produce a tough and even inedible bean. Some beans will come in and be ready for harvest all at once, like bush beans, so you might need to stagger the planting for these types.

Zinnias and Cauliflower

If you're not a fan of cauliflower, you can swap it out for any other member of the Brassica family. Regardless, zinnias and cauliflower make an excellent companion pairing. Cauliflower does need quite a bit of space since you want to grow more than one for cross-pollination reasons and because one cauliflower head is only worth some of the work you put in for months in advance.

Therefore, I would not recommend you plant this guild in a container, but you can grow it in a raised garden bed. Zinnias fit perfectly between the gaps of your cauliflower and will provide the most benefits this way, too.

Benefits

Of course, where there's a flower, there are beneficial insects like bees and butterflies, which will help with pest control and pollination for your edible garden crops. Zinnias are edible, by the way. They are on the bitter side but can still work well as decorations for cakes you made yourself or in a vase on display (for long-stemmed varieties). Zinnias also make great trap crops for common cauliflower pests.

Cauliflower doesn't have many benefits in the garden, but you can use the leaves and any scraps you cut off when preparing a meal as mulch (or to make fertilizer tea). Another overlooked benefit of cauliflower and zinnias is that they don't require much maintenance.

Care and Maintenance

Zinnias and cauliflower have similar growing requirements. They both like full sun and fertile, well-draining soil. Zinnias are warm-season flowers, while cauliflower is a cool-weather crop planted in spring after the last frost or fall. In frost-free climates, cauliflower is primarily grown in the winter, but you can cultivate it successfully all year round with some protection against frost or extreme heat.

While zinnias are hardy annuals and will likely take anything you throw at them, they are not very fond of the cold, so it's best to plant them in late spring or start them inside and transplant them after the last frost. Deadheading is the only maintenance needed for zinnias during the growing season—cutting off spent or withered flowers to encourage the plant to produce more. You should amend the soil once or twice with liquid fertilizer (or fertilizer tea) during the flowering period.

The key to growing cauliflower is consistent cool temperatures in the 60°F range, so timing is essential. Amend the soil with a generous amount of compost or other organic material in advance. Plant cauliflower seeds about a month before the last frost date. Add a thick layer of mulch over the soil (at least three inches) and water deeply once a week.

You might have to cover the seedlings with tunnel hoops or greenhouse structures to protect them from extreme cold (you can make your own with sturdy wire and plastic sheets as a more affordable option). It would help if you planted cauliflowers at least 18 inches apart.

Once the cauliflower heads are the size of golf balls, gently wrap the most prominent and extended surrounding leaves over the head and secure them with twine. This process is called blanching, and its purpose is to keep the cauliflower heads white since exposure to the sun will turn them yellow. Blanching cauliflower heads will also offer some protection against larger pests.

Fertilize your cauliflower every two weeks throughout the growing season by adding compost or liquid fertilizer around the base of the plant. Cauliflower is, after all, an annual, which means it's a heavy feeder. A good layer of mulch will suppress weeds, but if some manage to squeeze through, pull them out as soon as you notice them.

Harvesting

You can harvest zinnias when they open or like any other flower. But if you're using zinnias as trap crops, I recommend against eating them or using them as garnish or decorations for food items.

Harvesting cauliflower when it's big enough to eat but still compact (ideally when they're no less than six inches in diameter) would be best. Typically, this is around one week after you tie the leaves up and around the head. You can untie the leaves to check on the cauliflower head before harvesting. If it's still small and compact, you can leave it be for a few more days before checking again. If a cauliflower head looks like it wants to open up (the individual florets separate from each other), harvest it immediately, no matter the size, because the quality, texture, and taste will only worsen once this starts to happen.

Use a serrated knife to cut the cauliflower heads at the base of the neck, right below the leaves. You can leave the roots in the ground to decompose and release nutrients back into the soil; this is also good for underground microorganism populations.

If you take away one thing from this entire book, let it be this: It is probably easier than you think, and you will only succeed if you're willing to try and fail. Yes, it will require troubleshooting and learning from mistakes, but isn't that just life?

8

GARDENING IN SMALL SPACES

One of the biggest reasons many home gardeners never get into gardening despite their keen interest is the need for more planting space. Cultivating crops requires soil, water, light, and seeds.

Will a limited space have obstacles? Yes. Will you need to compromise on the type of crops and the amount you grow? Absolutely. But if your green thumb is itching, there is always a way to scratch it. This chapter reviews maximizing your growing space, even with zero outdoor space!

AVAILABLE SPACE

From a small grass-covered lawn to an apartment without as much as a front porch, companion planting, and permaculture principles have got you covered no matter how much space you have. Allow yourself to get creative with what you have right now instead of waiting for the right time to become an avid gardener.

Having enough space to grow whatever you want and as much as you want would be ideal, but life doesn't always work out that way. Let's look at the different sizes of planting space available to you and think of a few ways you can make it work regardless.

Smaller Gardens

You fall into this category if you have some in-ground garden bed to work with. This space could be a small grass patch or backyard where you could utilize the space more efficiently.

Grass is the standard for yards, but it's a waste of space. If you have a front or back yard with grass, you can replace it with a gardening space. This tactic is a viable option even if you're renting since all that you'll need to do to restore the yard to its original state is remove all crops, till the top layer of soil, sprinkle some grass seeds, and water regularly a few months before your lease is up.

The easiest way to convert a small grass garden into a usable gardening space is to mulch the entire area until the grass is dead; you can mulch with leaves, straw, cardboard, or all the above combined, as long as you cover every inch of grass in a thick layer. Water everything well and weekly. After a few months, you can till the top layer of soil, add compost, and start gardening.

Just make sure you plan your new garden space so you can still get around to everything (walkways, dividing spaces, etc.) Additionally, you can include other solutions yet to be discussed in this chapter to give yourself even more space to work with.

You will likely be able to grow almost anything you want in a small garden, but not as much as you want. A pro tip is to go for dwarf varieties to save space. Grow cherry tomatoes instead of regular ones, grow shallots or green onions instead of regular onions, and so on.

Concrete Only

In some instances, you may have a decent amount of space but no in-ground soil. This option includes oversized balconies, court-yards, or simply a paved (with bricks or concrete) front or back yard. You need soil for gardening, but no one said the soil must be in the ground.

For this problem, you can use raised garden beds directly on the concrete or container gardening. You can build your raised garden bed with wood or steel frames and corrugated iron as the siding.

Gardening on top of concrete or bricks might stain the concrete or leave a mark, even after power washing the site, which is not good news for renters. In this case, you can use old oil drums (or any other reusable, sizable containers) cut in half either lengthwise or crosswise (each half is decently sized). If you slice lengthwise, you must stabilize the drum with rocks, wood, or other ways. Remember to wash the containers well, make drainage holes, and round off any sharp edges for metal containers (use a wooden or rubber mallet to make the edges blunt or bent so you don't get cut).

As discussed earlier, bigger containers like oil drums, barrels, or small water tanks will offer you enough space to grow small guilds or companion pairings. However, you can also use ceramic pots, buckets, planters, or any other sizable containers you can get your hands on and arrange them accordingly right on top of the concrete. This option will bring some life and greenery into an otherwise very industrial and flat-looking space, plus you get to have some fresh produce on occasion.

You can treat a raised garden bed or container garden like you would an in-ground garden bed. This tactic means you can grow anything in it if the containers are big and deep enough.

Remember that you'll need to water crops growing in raised or container gardens more frequently.

Minimum Space

If you live in an urban area where you don't have much outdoor space, like in an apartment with a tiny balcony, porch, or micro garden, you can still make the most of it by growing crops that vine or climb or using vertical planters. You can make your vertical garden with PVC piping or gutters that you mount onto a wall or other structure. Of course, you can also buy vertical planters or make them out of wood if you have the financial means.

Even something as simple as a steel shelf can become a vertical planter. You can place individually potted crops on it and put your vining crops next to it so it uses the side of the shelf as support. Just make sure you arrange everything in such a way that they all get enough sunlight.

If you have a covered porch, attach a wire fence across one of the sides (preferably the one that gets the most sun) with some planters in front of it. You'll be able to grow beans, cucumbers, tomatoes, summer squash, and even grapes like this. Another thing you can do in addition to this is utilize hanging baskets.

Use the walls or ceiling when you don't have floor space! Grow up instead of out. Crops you can plant in hanging baskets include cherry tomatoes, strawberries, collard or leafy greens, cucumbers, and herbs.

No Outdoor Space

This scenario is by far the hardest to work around. Having absolutely no outdoor space is a hurdle. The only viable solution here is to grow everything indoors, similar to houseplants. You can grow many herbs in windowsills as long as sunlight reaches it.

This option will also limit the size of the plants. Opt for shade-tolerant and shallow-rooted crops, and invest in growth lights to grow fruiting crops (fruit and vegetables).

But the most challenging thing about growing your crops indoors is the lack of pollinators. You can open a window to let in a few bees to help themselves to your windowsill garden if you are okay with them, but this is only effective if there's not a lot of move-ment (insects typically avoid humans). Since only a few people want bees, wasps, and other insects in their homes, you have two options. Only grow self-fertile crops or hand-pollinate them.

Crops that will thrive in pots, indoors, and with a bit of help from a growth lamp include microgreens, carrots, beets, radishes, onions, chives, garlic, thyme, mint, parsley, rosemary, peppers, and leafy greens.

MINIMALIST GARDENING

Earlier, we discussed how you should only grow crops you will use and eat. When you have minimum space, you don't have a choice in this regard. Every inch counts and must be used to its fullest potential.

A good starting point is to list all the fruits and vegetables you and your family eat regularly and cross out any incompatable for your garden space scenario or skill level. For example, you won't be able to grow a peach tree indoors. But you might be able to grow basil.

Don't tell anyone I said this, but ditch the flowers if necessary. They take up a lot of space, and besides a few outliers, the only real benefit most of them offer is aesthetics, attracting pollinators, and being used as trap crops, which is excellent if you have the space for it. Most fruit and vegetable crops have flowers anyway, which does an excellent job of attracting beneficial insects. You can use other crops and herbs to help keep pests at bay (and it's more functional and minimalistic).

Another thing to consider is quantity over price point. Growing potatoes takes up a lot of space and is very unpredictable. You might end up with marble-sized potatoes and months of wasted time and space. If you're not breaking your budget buying potatoes and onions at the store, buy them and grow something you like but can only sometimes buy because it's expensive (like strawberries).

FAST-PACED GARDENING

Time is a precious resource, and when you don't have much space to grow your produce, you need to raise as much as possible as quickly as possible. Instead of growing crops that need to grow and become established for a year before fruiting, go for quick-growing crops that will bear produce in a few months.

Succession planting and intercropping are non-negotiable when gardening space is limited. Growing something every season and planting companion crops together will ensure no space goes to waste. This approach and quick-producing crops will give you the best bang for your buck.

Here's a list of common vegetables and herbs that will mature and be ready for harvest within mere weeks or months of being sowed:

- Microgreens (two weeks).
- Beets (two months).
- Spinach (one month).
- Radishes (one month).
- Green beans (two months).
- Mustard greens (one month).
- Arugula and rocket (two months).
- Green onions (one month).
- Cucumbers (three months).
- Spring onions (three months).
- Mint (three months).
- Basil (two months).

We're gardeners. We do what we can with what we have. We're resilient, creative, and life-givers. Don't let a lack of outdoor space stop you from enjoying what you love or being surrounded by greenery and fresh produce.

9

COMPANION PLANTING AND PEST CONTROL

T he second chapter discussed how certain plants (usually herbs and flowers) help with natural pest management. Some give off a strong scent that disguises crops or confuses pests; others attract predatory insects that eat the pests or their eggs and offspring. And in some cases, some plants are sacrificed as trap crops for the good of our food source.

The approach that will give you the best results is a comprehensive one that has aspects of all the above characteristics: either a single crop type for pest control that has a fragrant but undesirable scent and flowers for attracting predatory insects or a crop type for each of these (a strong-scented herb, a flowering plant, and a trap crop) in the same guild. This approach is sometimes possible, but some protection is better than none.

Managing pests with companion planting is possible, but it's not the only solution. You'll still have pests (you're putting food in their natural habitat; after all, we can't blame them for being hungry), but their populations won't be out of control to the point where all your crops will get ruined. In this chapter, we'll be going into more detail on which plants help keep common garden pests in check.

COMMON GARDEN PESTS AND WHAT TO PLANT

You will encounter a few common pests no matter where you set up your garden. You must know how to identify them and what to do about them. This section will review the most common garden pests, what crops they typically look for, and what you should plant to deter them.

Spider Mites

Spider mites are tiny, spider-like pests (almost microscopic at 1/50 of an inch when fully grown). Yes, they look like spiders (even fall under the arachnid species) and are most commonly red, orange, or brown. They suck the sap out of new foliage growth and live on the underside of leaves that are in direct sun. Spider mites leave behind webs on the bottom of the leaves they've inhabited (how they got their names), and despite being so small, they can deliver a lot of damage.

Planting cilantro, dill, and fennel will attract ladybugs, which will help keep spider mite populations in check, and strangely enough, thrips also snack on these tiny spiders (a pest feeding on a pest, how ironic). But if you're dealing with an infestation of spider mites, you can spray isopropyl alcohol on your leaves (be sure to get the bottoms especially), giving them a killer hangover; emphasis on the "killer."

Aphids

These creatures are about the size of a pinhead (once they reach adulthood) and pear-shaped, but some species of aphids can grow substantially larger (like the Giant Willow Aphid). But for the sake of naming common pests, we're only referencing the small, soft-bodied, and pear-shaped ones present in most gardens worldwide. Aphids can be any color, but most commonly, they are white, black, brown, green, or yellow with a waxy or hairy coating. They can also grow wings in adulthood.

Aphids like hanging out on the underside of leaves and will also be on the stems. Their primary source of sustenance is the sap, which they drink from the leaves and stems of young crops or new growth. In large quantities, aphids can have devastating consequences for your fruits, vegetables, and flowers.

When I say aphids don't discriminate against crops, they will camp on nearly every fruiting or flowering crop you have. You can manage aphid populations with scent and predatory insects (specifically ladybugs and their larvae, which actively feed on aphids).

Aphids aren't attracted to garlic, chives, catnip, cilantro, or marigolds, so planting these around the garden (especially near your fruiting crops) will help. In addition, the marigold and cilantro attract ladybugs and shelter them: two birds, one stone.

Thrips

Another tiny menace. Thrips grow to be about (1 mm.) in length, are long and slender, and have underdeveloped wings that allow them to fly for short distances. The color of thrips ranges between green, yellow, brown, and amber, and adults have an orange thorax (chest area). Similarly, they feed on a plant's sap, which you can find on the leaves' underside. They usually don't stay long; by the time you see the damage, they're usually gone (they move in large groups). However, they might leave behind "evidence" in the form of tiny black spots.

The damage they leave behind can be stunted growth, dying (or yellowing) leaves, reduced yield, fruit scarring, and can even lead to the death of some plants. They often attack seedlings, new plant growth, flowers (and blossoms), and fruits.

Basil, garlic, chives, and catnip seem to do a good job keeping thrips away; however, for maximum protection, you can also lure their natural predators into the garden (lacewings, ladybirds, and wasps) by growing goldenrod, yarrow, yellow coneflowers, and flowering herbs.

Whitefly

Whiteflies are a bit easier to spot since they are larger (1-2mm.) The bodies of whiteflies are yellowish, but their wings are white and covered in a powdery substance. If there are a lot of whiteflies on a plant, you may notice a swarm of them flying right above the area. They cause damage in the same way that aphids and thrips do by sucking the juices out of your crops' leaves and stems.

Plants under stress will be more susceptible to a whitefly infestation, but they will also attack all sorts of fruit, vegetables, shrubs, herbs, and flower crops. They cause what's known as "sooty mold," which may kill the plant. Whiteflies hate marigolds, and you can further manage them with predatory wasps and beetles. You can attract these insects by planting alyssum, dill, rosemary, or any plant in the carrot family around your precious crops.

Leaf Miners

This pest isn't necessarily a specific type of insect but rather the larvae of numerous insects such as moths, flies, and some beetles. In essence, leaf miners are just babies but can still damage crops. What happens is moths, flies, beetles, and the like will lay their eggs inside the leaves of your crops. When these eggs hatch, the larvae will bore their way out of the leaves, leaving behind white or yellow squiggly lines on the leaves.

If you see these white or yellow lines (it's pretty hard to miss), you know leaf miners were there. It's rare for leaf miners to cause severe damage to a plant; in most cases, the leaf will turn brown and fall off prematurely. However, severe infestations can leave the plant weak and susceptible to other pests and diseases, leading to the plant's death.

To minimize the chance of such an infestation, you can plant a variety of mint, lavender, marigold, thyme, cloves, and bay leaves around your garden, which will keep flies, moths, and other insects away.

Snails and Slugs

These slimy suckers are not picky when it comes to food and will eat anything in sight, including meat, waste, decaying matter, and even cardboard. They go crazy for leafy greens, so you'll usually find them amongst your lettuce patch, but they will not hesitate to invade berries and anything else you have growing. If it has leaves, they will make a meal out of it.

Snails and homeless snails (slugs) hate the smell and taste of mint and garlic (or even onions and chives, for that matter). To keep these pests away, plant either mint or garlic all around the border of your garden bed (raised or in-ground). Alternatively, you can dig a border around your in-ground garden bed and fill it with pebbles or sand (they don't like these textures), but this method could be more effective.

10

COMPANION PLANTING FOR DIFFERENT CLIMATES

I'm sure you know by now that different crops grow in different seasons, like cauliflower, a cool-season crop, whereas peppers are a warm-season crop. But your climate will also severely impact the type of crops you grow. Seasons look different depending on the environment.

CLIMATE ZONES

A climate combines a specific region's long-term average temperature, humidity, and precipitation (rainfall) levels. There are many different climates, but all of them can fit into five distinct categories of climate zones. In this section, we'll cover all these climates, their seasons, and which companion pairs thrive best in each one.

Tropical

Tropical climates are known for hot and humid weather. With an average minimum temperature of 64 °F (even in winter) and at least 60 inches of rainfall per year, tropical climates are perfect for almost any crop because there are no winters. Examples of tropical regions include Mexico, Central America, the Caribbean Islands, the top half of South America, and the Amazon rainforest.

Most famously, tropical climates are known for growing the best coconuts, pineapples, bananas, melons, gourds, grapefruit, mango, cashews, avocados, and guava, to name a few. You can grow these crops in other regions, but they tend to do best in tropical climates.

Some great companion pairs to grow in tropical climates include:

- Beets and broccoli.
- Bananas and sweet potatoes.
- Mango tree and nasturtiums.
- Eggplant and spinach.
- Avocado tree and garlic.
- Pumpkin (or squash) and chamomile.

Temperate

Regions or countries that fall under this climate have warm and humid summers with mild winters (typically without frost or snow). The average summer temperatures for temperate climates are above 50 °F, with the coldest months not falling below 37 °F. Due to the stable nature of this climate, you can easily overwinter your crops and get a more extended harvest period.

Some examples of countries that have temperate climates are the United Kingdom, Japan, North Africa, and most of Europe. Almost all crops can be grown in temperate regions. Because temperate climates are in the middle of the extremes when it comes to temperatures (it's never too cold or too hot), you can grow any companion guild or pair successfully.

Continental

This climate includes warm summers but frigid, snowy winters (as cold as -22 °F). Examples of continental climate regions include most of Russia, northern and northeastern China, central Canada, and some parts of the north of the United States.

You'll likely be able to grow a large variety of crops in a continental summer, fall, and spring. However, you will only be able to produce a little in winter unless you have a greenhouse (and even then, some crops that are sensitive to frost might suffer).

As mentioned, you can grow almost anything in continental climates. Still, I recommend starting your crops indoors or in a greenhouse as early as possible. Hence, your harvest period comes sooner since overwintering (letting crops continue to produce into early winter) is not an option.

Dry

This zone is self-explanatory, but dry climates are areas that receive less than 16 inches of rainfall per year and are known to be hot and dry (desert-like). Some examples include the Sahara Desert, Australia, and most of the southwestern United States.

Dry climates are the hardest to work with when it comes to gardening. It's not impossible to grow crops here, but there are limitations. You must put effort into your gardening setup and implement preventive methods to protect your crops from extreme heat and lack of rain. For example, raised garden beds or containers, shade netting, thick mulch, and more frequent irrigation are necessary in a dry climate.

Aloe and agave are succulents, work well in dry climates, and are great options for in-ground landscaping. However, there's little you can do with aloe and agave. Instead, your best defense will be to grow drought-tolerant crops and put measures (as mentioned above) in place to prevent your crops from dying. Here's a list of companion pairs that work well in dry climates:

- Rhubarb and cowpeas.
- Peppers and basil. (Basil is quite drought tolerant once established.)
- Lavender and alliums.
- Grapes and oregano.
- Zucchini and radish. (Once established, both these are pretty drought tolerant.)
- Swiss chard and chives.

Polar

The constant frozen state is a defining characteristic of polar climates. The average temperature in a polar environment is below freezing, and ice and snow always cover the landscape. They don't get direct sun heat for 50% of the year. Polar climates only occur around the northern and southern parts of the world (the North Pole and Antarctica).

Because of the extreme cold and icy conditions, growing anything outdoors in a polar climate is very hard. Even the hardiest crops and trees struggle to survive the freezing temperatures without artificial sunlight (growth lamps of UV light), heat, and complete shelter.

Besides a select few variants of mosses, lichens, and Arctic Poppies, nothing else grows naturally in polar climates. If you can manage to create the right conditions through greenhouses, growth lamps, heaters, and what have you, you'll likely be able to grow a variety of cold-tolerant crops, including:

- Spinach and peas.
- Carrots and onions.
- Cauliflower and cabbage.
- Garlic and turnips.

Knowing which climate you're in, like the back of your hand, will help you develop a better game plan when planning your guilds and pairings. Set yourself up for success by researching your climate, zone, and seasonal changes and planning your gardening schedule. It's so much easier to stay on top of everything when you know what plants thrive in your climate when to sow, and how long it will take before you can harvest.

11

TROUBLESHOOTING AND TIPS

No matter your skill level, years of experience, or research abilities, you will come across a gardening obstacle now and then. The good news is that by taking preventative action, you minimize this, and with the information in this chapter, you can overcome almost any problem that arises.

PREVENTATIVE MEASURES

Poor soil quality and inadequate planning are the most common gardening problems discouraging many novice gardeners. If you plant a seed, it will most likely sprout but only last for a while. To reach maturity (and produce a harvest), you must give it what it needs from the start.

You must take, implement, or consider preventative measures long before cultivating anything. These include:

- Amending the Soil.

Have your soil thoroughly tested, or use an at-home soil test kit. Based on the test results, add compost, fertilizer, mulch, sand, clay, ash, or anything else your soil might need. A healthy and productive garden starts with soil quality. You should amend the soil at least a few months before planting or sowing to give the soil some time to stabilize and grow beneficial microorganism populations.

- Considering the Climate You're In.

Growing crops unsuitable to your specific environment is possible, but such plants require much more rigorous maintenance and observation. You'll only make it much harder to keep your garden alive and end up with underperforming or inadequate harvests.

- Using Adjusted Seeds and Seedlings.

When buying seeds or seedlings, it's always better to buy those cultivated in and around your area because they will have specific resistance to your weather and climate conditions. For example, imported seeds will have a more challenging time adjusting and thriving than seeds or seedlings from a local lineage.

- Planning Your Guilds.

Certain plants get along well with each other, while others will result in catastrophe for your garden if planted together. Plan your guilds based on the best companions, their basic needs, the space they will take up, and other maintenance requirements.

AVOIDING COMMON GARDENING PROBLEMS

Pests, diseases, overcrowding, stripped soil. How do you avoid these gardening problems? And better yet, how do you fix the problem once you notice it? As I said, even if you do everything right, you still need the answers to these questions.

You should monitor your garden regularly to see signs of a potential problem rearing its head. To make this more efficient and effective, you can keep a garden journal where you record notes and observations on the general health of your plants. You can also write down any adjustments you should make to fertilization dates, planting schedules, etc. With gardening, there's almost always a lot to consider; you will only remember something if you write it down.

Nevertheless, here's a list of some common gardening issues and how to prevent or correct them:

- Pests and Diseases.

Never having pests or diseases is an unattainable goal when gardening. The goal is minimization and early intervention. Companion planting and intercropping will drastically reduce the chance of your garden spreading infection, disease, and suffering from pest infestations, but you should keep an eye on things.

If you notice more pests lurking around your garden than what is deemed "normal," you can step in and give your garden some external help by using things like netting, neem oil, traps or trap crops, and other non-chemical methods. In severe cases, unfortunately, you might have to discard the infested or infected plants entirely.

- Small Yields.

When a crop is underperforming, the resulting fruit might be smaller, or the plant may produce less than average. Factors such as disease, pests, genetic mutations, poor soil quality, lack of pollinators, or unmet basic needs and requirements could cause underperformance.

A comprehensive approach might be needed to determine what the problem is. Double-check that you meet the plant's essential water, sun, and soil requirements. Inspect the plant thoroughly for any signs of pests or disease. Then, amend the soil with liquid fertilizer and take action to invite pollinators to your garden (plant more flowering crops).

Another thing contributing to a poor yield is not letting the plant become established before allowing it to flower and fruit. Remember to pinch off the flower buds (for some perennial crops) in the first year so the plant can become more established —an adequately set plant will produce bigger and better quality fruit.

- Poor Soil Quality.

Your soil quality will depend on the crops you are planting and how often you feed the soil. You are likely stripping the soil if you mainly grow annuals (heavy feeders) but only add compost or fertilizer once a year. The soil quality will quickly deteriorate if you're not protecting the ground from the elements using mulch or living mulch. Not to mention, your soil will dry out quicker and leave your crops thirsty.

Not rotating crops (or not doing it correctly) will also result in the degradation of the quality of your soil.

- Overcrowding.

Always follow the general guidelines on how far apart you should plant crops from each other. These guidelines are there for a reason. Overcrowding can result in many problems, including poor yields, stunted growth, diseases, pests, and increased competition for nutrients. Find other ways to maximize space instead of overcrowding your garden.

If your garden is overcrowded, start by thinning out the most miniature, least productive plants and filling in the gaps with mulch or ground cover crops.

- Overwatering.

I am trying to remember where I read this rule, but I've been living by it for as long as I can remember: It's not about the quantity of water, but the frequency. If you have well-draining soil, it's almost impossible to give a plant too much water at once; the soil will absorb as much as it can, and the rest will drain away.

Don't get me wrong, overwatering a plant might cause some issues, like diluting or washing away essential nutrients and microorganisms, so you should water them sparingly. But the key is in how frequently you water your crops. It would help if you always allowed the soil to dry out a little before you water again, which is why most established plants only require you to water them once a week. Aim to saturate the top two or three inches thoroughly.

Overwatering can result in degrading the quality of the soil and root rot and might even suffocate your roots. Signs you might be overwatering include loss of old and new foliage, wilting leaves, or gray, slimy roots. To correct this, remove and repot the plant in a large enough container with very loose and well-draining soil (add pebbles or vermiculite to aid drainage and air pockets). Wait to water the plant until the top layer of soil is completely dry.

- Bolting.

Bolting refers to premature seeding (the plant switches from fruiting to seed production before it's supposed to). Especially when temperatures are too high, the plant can experience early seeding due to not meeting its basic needs.

Try amending the soil with fertilizer and moving the plant (or guild) to an area that receives partial shade. Alternatively, you can create a structure to shade the plant from the harsh afternoon sun.

As time goes on, you'll learn all the tricks and trades of gardening. You can only learn some things through experience and time. I only ask that you stay committed and not let a few hiccups stop you from doing what you love.

Inspire a Fellow Gardener!

You picked up this book because you love gardens and you wanted to build your own… so I know you're on board with helping more gardens flourish. This is your chance to inspire another new gardener.

Simply by sharing your honest opinion of this book and a little about your own gardening journey, you'll show new readers where they can find a clear route to gardening success.

LEAVE A REVIEW!

Thank you so much for your support. I wish you many years of happiness in your garden.

Scan the QR code below to leave a review:

CONCLUSION

The answer to the question, "Why should I implement companion planting?" is simple but lengthy. Everyone will have a different reason for starting and following this permaculture principle. But companion planting is like a one-stop shop to cultivate a thriving, eco-friendly, diverse garden.

Nature has always found a way to persevere. Savvy gardeners know trying and going against Mother Nature's will is pointless. It's the responsibility of all humans to look after what we have. We share the planet with many other creatures, many of which were here long before we came along.

Whether people believe companion planting works is irrelevant, not only because many studies have proven it is effective and beneficial, but because it's simply the way things are. Despite not having any maintenance or human intervention, forests, grass-lands, valleys, and open fields survive. No, they thrive!

We're simply conforming to the natural laws. When you let nature do its thing, it benefits every living thing around it. You might have to deal with bugs, pests, weeds, and diseases, but they all play a valuable role in the grand scheme. Using pesticides, insecticides, and chemical fertilizers does more harm than good. Not only does it eliminate the weeds and pests, but it also negatively impacts every other creature that comes into contact with these harmful toxins.

I'm certainly not one to preach about only buying organic produce or going entirely off the grid. But if you do want fresh, organic, and non-GMO produce that genuinely leaves the environment better off, the best way to ensure that's what you're getting is to grow it yourself.

If you're starting with companion planting (or gardening in general), you'll likely need some help. Every mistake or failure is an opportunity to become better at something, to learn, to experiment. Losing a plant you've worked hard to keep alive can be demotivating; having an entire batch of seedlings succumb to "dampening off" is devastating, and dealing with pest infestations is frustrating beyond belief. But don't think of it as time wasted; think of it as experience gained.

Planning the perfect guild according to your needs, situation, and climate takes time, creativity, and more research than you'll ever do in your entire life. But when you get it right, few things in life beat that kind of satisfaction, confidence, and pride.

And that's what inspired me to write this book. I wanted to give you a head start and make it more attainable. To put you in the thick of it, getting hands-on experience without all the potential things that can go wrong when you plan your guild.

So, whether you have a decently sized backyard or nothing but a windowsill, I hope you find it in you to at least try to make it work. Even if all you get out of it are fresh chives to put on instant noodles. It's the action that inspires motivation, not the other way around.

With the knowledge you have gained from this book, transform your space into a self-sustaining ecosystem with its circle of life. Keep pests, weeds, and diseases under control, and reap the benefits of an all-natural, minimal-maintenance garden. And remember to be patient with yourself and your crops.

REFERENCES

Adamant, A. (2018, August 23). *How to grow chives*. Practical Self Reliance. https://practicalselfreliance.com/growing-chives/

Albert, S. (2022, June 8). *How to plant, grow, and harvest cilantro*. Harvest to Table. https://harvesttotable.com/how_to_grow_coriander_and_cila/

Amendolare, N. (2023, November 21). *Climate zones: Definitions, types, and examples*. Study.com. https://study.com/learn/lesson/climate-zones-geography-types.html

Amy. (2015, July 20). *5 Reasons to grow chives*. Tenth Acre Farm. https://www.tenthacrefarm.com/5-reasons-to-grow-chives/

Amy. (2017, May 18). *12 Steps to preventing garden pests naturally*. Tenth Acre Farm. https://www.tenthacrefarm.com/preventing-garden-pests/

Anderson, T. (2020, September 25). *The easiest way to test soil pH and amend it*. Lovely Greens. https://lovelygreens.com/easiest-way-test-soil-ph/

Arcuri, L. (2021, September 23). *Everything you need to know about growing garlic*. The Spruce. https://www.thespruce.com/grow-great-garlic-3016629

Baessler, L. (2015, September 29). *Container grown grapes: Tips for planting grapevines in pots*. Gardening Know How. https://www.gardeningknowhow.com/edible/fruits/grapes/container-grown-grapes.htm#:

Balogh, A. (2019). *Caring for roses: A beginner's rose growing guide*. Garden Design. https://www.gardendesign.com/roses/care.html

Ben Issa, R., Gautier, H., & Gomez, L. (2016). Influence of neighbouring companion plants on the performance of aphid populations on sweet pepper plants under greenhouse conditions. *Agricultural and Forest Entomology*, *19*(2), 131–191. https://doi.org/10.1111/afe.12199

Ben-Issa, R., Gomez, L., & Gautier, H. (2017). Companion plants for aphid pest management. *Insects*, *8*(4), 112. https://doi.org/10.3390/insects8040112

Blooming Backyard. (2021, November 11). *10 Rosemary companion plants (& 5 plants to keep far away)*. https://www.bloomingbackyard.com/rosemary-companion-plants/

Boeckmann, C. (2019, June 11). *Cucumbers*. Old Farmer's Almanac. https://www.almanac.com/plant/cucumbers

Bonnie Plants. (n.d.). *How to grow cauliflower in your garden*. Bonnie Plants. https://bonnieplants.com/blogs/how-to-grow/growing-cauliflower#:

Brillon, K. (2023, August 1). *17 Companion plants to grow with beets*. Epic Gardening. https://www.epicgardening.com/beet-companion-plants/

Cason, K. (2022, April 20). *The benefits of marigolds in your vegetable garden*. Senior Living Magazine. https://seniorlivingmag.co.za/2022/04/20/the-benefits-of-marigolds-in-your-vegetable-garden/#:

Chen, L., Li, D., Shao, Y., Adni, J., Wang, H., Liu, Y., & Zhang, Y. (2020). Comparative analysis of soil microbiome profiles in the companion planting of white clover and orchard grass using 16S rRNA gene sequencing data. *Frontiers in Plant Science, 11*, 538311. https://doi.org/10.3389/fpls.2020.538311

Cheng, F., & Cheng, Z. (2015). Research progress on the use of plant allelopathy in agriculture and the physiological and ecological mechanisms of allelopathy. *Frontiers, 6*. https://www.frontiersin.org/articles/10.3389/fpls.2015.01020/full

Dore, J. (2010, June 4). *Trap cropping to control pests*. GrowVeg. https://www.growveg.com/guides/trap-cropping-to-control-pests/

Durant, J. (2023, March 16). *How to grow parsley: A comprehensive guide*. Natural Seed-Bank. https://www.seed-bank.ca/how-to-grow-parsley-companion-planting/

Dylan. (2023, May 24). *The 11 best companion plants for oregano*. Make It Seasonal. https://makeitseasonal.com/oregano-companion-plants/

Ellis, M. E. (2022, March 22). *History of companion planting – how did companion planting start*. Gardening Know How. https://blog.gardeningknowhow.com/tbt/history-of-companion-planting/

Engels, J. (2016, August 22). *Guilds for the small scale home garden*. The Permaculture Research Institute. https://www.permaculturenews.org/2016/08/22/guilds-small-scale-home-garden/

Fu, X., Li, C., Zhou, X., Liu, S., & Wu, F. (2016). Physiological response and sulfur metabolism of the V. dahliae-infected tomato plants in tomato/potato onion companion cropping. *Scientific Reports, 6*(1). https://doi.org/10.1038/srep36445

Fuss, C. (2021, August 30). *Pepper companion plants: Produce pals*. Epic Gardening. https://www.epicgardening.com/pepper-companion-plants/#:

Gao, J., & Zhang, F. (2023). Influence of companion planting on microbial compositions and their symbiotic network in pepper continuous cropping soil. *Journal of Microbiology and Biotechnology, 33*(6), 760–770. https://doi.org/10.4014/jmb.2211.11032

Gardeners' World. (n.d.). *How to grow borage*. https://www.gardenersworld.com/how-to/grow-plants/how-to-grow-borage/

Gardeners' World. (2019, February 26). *How to grow zinnias*. BBC Gardeners World Magazine. https://www.gardenersworld.com/how-to/grow-plants/how-to-grow-zinnias/

Georgina. (n.d.). *Planting, growing and harvesting green beans*. https://www.georgina.

ca/sites/default/files/page_assets/planting_growing_harvesting_green_bean s.pdf

Gibson, A. (2017, September 6). *5 Reasons to grow sunflowers.* The Micro Gardener. https://themicrogardener.com/5-benefits-reasons-to-grow-sunflowers/#:

Grant, A. (2023, September 3). *Best companion plants for thyme in the garden.* Gardening Know How. https://www.gardeningknowhow.com/edible/herbs/thyme/thyme-companions.htm

Griffiths-Lee, J., Nicholls, E., & Goulson, D. (2020). Companion planting to attract pollinators increases the yield and quality of strawberry fruit in gardens and allotments. *Ecological Entomology, 45*(5), 1025–1034. https://doi.org/10.1111/een.12880

Grow Forage Cook Ferment. (2020, May 25). *10 Reasons to grow oregano: A highly beneficial herb.* Grow Forage Cook Ferment. https://www.growforagecookferment.com/benefits-of-oregano/#:

Gupta, S. (2010). Chamomile: A herbal medicine of the past with a bright future (review). *Molecular Medicine Reports, 3*(6). https://doi.org/10.3892/mmr.2010.377

Habas, C. (2012, April 6). *How to plant onions next to other vegetables.* Weekand. https://www.weekand.com/home-garden/article/plant-onions-next-other-vegetables-18057809.php

Hailey, L. (2022a, April 29). *31 Strawberry companion plants to grow with strawberries.* Epic Gardening. https://www.epicgardening.com/strawberry-companion-plants/

Hailey, L. (2022b, September 28). *15 Tips for vegetable gardening in small spaces.* Epic Gardening. https://www.epicgardening.com/gardening-limited-space/

Hassani, N. (2021, November 29). *The basics of companion planting garden crops.* The Spruce. https://www.thespruce.com/companion-planting-with-chart-5025124

Haynes, G. (2023, May 13). *How to grow and care for sunflowers.* Southern Living. https://www.southernliving.com/garden/flowers/how-to-grow-sunflowers#:

Healthy Living. (n.d.). *The power of parsley.* Healthy Living. https://healthyliving-herbs.co.za/the-power-of-parsley/#:

Hicks-Hamblin, K. (2021, September 29). *The benefits of companion planting.* Gardener's Path. https://gardenerspath.com/how-to/organic/benefits-companion-planting/

Hughes, R. A. (2023, April 2). *What noise does a plant make when it's under stress?* Euronews. https://www.euronews.com/green/2023/04/02/scientists-have-recorded-the-sound-plants-make-when-they-are-under-stress

Iannotti, M. (2022a, June 23). *Easy to grow comfrey wildflowers.* The Spruce. https://www.thespruce.com/growing-comfrey-1402605

Iannotti, M. (2022b, July 29). *How to grow fragrant lavender*. The Spruce. https://www.thespruce.com/growing-lavender-1402779#:

Iannotti, M. (2022c, July 31). *How to grow rosemary indoors and out*. The Spruce. https://www.thespruce.com/grow-and-care-for-rosemary-plants-1403406

Iannotti, M. (2022d, August 20). *How to grow and care for chamomile*. The Spruce. https://www.thespruce.com/how-to-grow-chamomile-1402627

Iannotti, M. (2023, March 18). *How to grow blueberries at home*. The Spruce. https://www.thespruce.com/growing-blueberries-1401960

Insect Science. (2020a, July 7). *How to identify and get rid of aphids on garden plants naturally*. Home and Garden. https://shop.insectscience.co.za/garden-pests/aphids/

Insect Science. (2020b, July 8). *How to identify and get rid of thrips pests in your garden*. Home and Garden. https://shop.insectscience.co.za/garden-pests/thrips/

Insect Science. (2020c, July 8). *How to identify and get rid of whiteflies on houseplants*. Home and Garden. https://shop.insectscience.co.za/garden-pests/white-fly/

Insect Science. (2020d, July 10). *How to identify and control leaf miners naturally | insect science*. Home and Garden. https://shop.insectscience.co.za/garden-pests/leaf-miner/

Jill. (2019, October 29). *Crop rotation for home vegetable gardeners*. The Beginner's Garden. https://journeywithjill.net/gardening/2019/10/28/crop-rotation-for-home-vegetable-gardeners/

Johnson, Zach. *Garden Quotes We Love*. Maryland Plant Nursery & Garden Center in Bowie, MD | Patuxent Nursery. Last modified March 14, 2023. https://patuxentnursery.com/blog/garden-quotes-we-love/

Kanuckel, A. (2018, April 25). *Companion planting guide: Sow easy*. Old Farmers' Almanac. https://www.farmersalmanac.com/companion-planting-guide

Khait, I., Lewin-Epstein, O., Sharon, R., Saban, K., Goldstein, R., Anikster, Y., Zeron, Y., Agassy, C., Nizan, S., Sharabi, G., Perelman, R., Boonman, A., Sade, N., Yovel, Y., & Hadany, L. (2023). Sounds emitted by plants under stress are airborne and informative. *Cell, 186*(7), 1328-1336.e10. https://doi.org/10.1016/j.cell.2023.03.009

Kong, C.-H., Xuan, T. D., Khanh, T. D., Tran, H.-D., & Trung, N. T. (2019). Allelochemicals and Signaling Chemicals in Plants. *Molecules, 24*(15). https://doi.org/10.3390/molecules24152737

Landers, L. (2023, September 2). *What is a permaculture garden? Plus how to plant your own*. Better Homes & Gardens. https://www.bhg.com/what-is-a-permaculture-garden-7775333

Larum, D. (n.d.). *Companions for chamomile*. Gardening Know How.com. https://www.gardeningknowhow.com/edible/herbs/chamomile/chamomile-plant-companions.htm

Living Seeds. (n.d.). *Companion planting.* https://livingseeds.co.za/companion-planti ng.html

Love The Garden. (n.d.-a). *How to grow and care for sage.* https://www.lovethegar den.com/au-en/growing-guide/how-grow-care-sage

Love The Garden. (n.d.-b). *How to grow apple trees.* https://www.lovethegarden.com/ au-en/growing-guide/how-grow-care-apple-trees#:

Magyar, C. (2021, February 10). *Bad neighbors - the ultimate guide to incompatible companion plants.* Rural Sprout. https://www.ruralsprout.com/incompatible-companion-plants/

Mane. (2021, April 30). *How to prune fruit trees in 8 steps.* Mehrabyan Nursery. https://www.mehrabyannursery.com/growing-guide/fruit-trees/how-to-prune-fruit-trees/

McCauley, T. (2023, July 6). *Companion planting: 43 Combinations for maximum yield.* https://www.tiffanymccauley.com/companion-planting/

Montoya, J. E., Arnold, M. A., Rangel, J., Stein, L. R., & Palma, M. A. (2020). Pollinator-attracting companion plantings increase crop yield of cucumbers and habanero peppers. *HortScience, 55*(2), 164–169. https://doi.org/10.21273/ hortsci14468-19

Morini, R. (2023, February). *Biodiversity: Its meaning, importance and how home gardeners can help restore it.* Piedmont Master Gardeners. https://piedmontmas tergardeners.org/article/biodiversity-its-meaning-importance-and-how-home-gardeners-can-help-restore-it/

Moulton, M. (2022, March 2). *12 Sunflower companion plants (& 3 plants to grow nowhere near).* Blooming Backyard. https://www.bloomingbackyard.com/ sunflower-companion-plants/

New Mexico State University. (2015). *Propagation of grape vine cuttings: A practical guide | new mexico state university - BE BOLD. shape the future.* Pubs.nmsu.edu. https://pubs.nmsu.edu/_h/H322/index.html#:

Old Farmer's Almanac. (2019a, April 17). *Peaches.* https://www.almanac.com/plant/ peaches

Old Farmer's Almanac. (2019b, April 22). *Chives.* https://www.almanac.com/plant/ chives

Old Farmer's Almanac. (2019c, October 28). *The three sisters: Corn, beans, and squash.* https://www.almanac.com/content/three-sisters-corn-bean-and-squash

Oregon State University. (2010, June 4). *Rhododendrons and azaleas need a strong acidic soil.* Extension Communications. https://extension.oregonstate.edu/ news/rhododendrons-azaleas-need-strong-acidic-soil

Pammy. (2014, January 29). *TSG: Companion planting: Petunias love beans.* TSG. https://thymesquaregarden.blogspot.com/2014/01/companion-planting-petu nias-love-beans.html?m=1

Park Seed. (n.d.). *The-ultimate-guide-to-companion-planting-vegetables.* https://park seed.com/guide-to-companion-planting-vegetables/a/the-ultimate-guide-to-companion-planting-vegetables/

Peerless, V. (2021, November 8). *How to grow and care for nasturtiums.* BBC Gardeners World Magazine. https://www.gardenersworld.com/how-to/grow-plants/how-to-grow-nasturtiums/#harvesting

Plant Perfect. (2022, March 28). *How to design the perfect vegetable garden layout.* https://plantperfect.com/how-to-design-the-perfect-vegetable-garden-layout/

Pleasant, B. (2013). *Growing and harvesting garden dill.* GrowVeg. https://www.growveg.co.za/guides/growing-and-harvesting-garden-dill/

Rahbardar, M., & Hosseinzadeh, H. (2020). Therapeutic effects of rosemary (Rosmarinus officinalis L.) and its active constituents on nervous system disorders. *Therapeutic Effects of Rosemary (Rosmarinus Officinalis L.) and Its Active Constituents on Nervous System Disorders, 23*(9). https://doi.org/10.22038/ijbms.2020.45269.10541

Raman, R. (2018, February 22). *Cilantro vs coriander: What's the difference?* Healthline. https://www.healthline.com/nutrition/cilantro-vs-coriander#:

Restoration Seeds. (n.d.). *Germinating perennial seeds.* https://www.restorationseeds.com/blogs/news/7211932-germinating-perennial-seeds

Riesselman, L. (n.d.). *Companion planting: A method for sustainable pest control RFR-A9099.* https://dr.lib.iastate.edu/server/api/core/bitstreams/9f6c0efd-b8b1-4ecc-b8d1-2abbdfb16548/content#:

Saldanha, A. V., Gontijo, L. M., Carvalho, R. M. R., Vasconcelos, C. J., Corrêa, A. S., & Gandra, R. L. R. (2019). Companion planting enhances pest suppression despite reducing parasitoid emergence. *Basic and Applied Ecology, 41,* 45–55. https://doi.org/10.1016/j.baae.2019.10.002

Scavo, A., Abbate, C., & Mauromicale, G. (2019). Plant allelochemicals: Agronomic, nutritional and ecological relevance in the soil system. *Plant and Soil.* https://doi.org/10.1007/s11104-019-04190-y

Sciortino, D. G. (2023, September 3). *Cucumber is the secret weapon you need for a happy and healthy garden.* House Digest. https://www.housedigest.com/1381567/cucumber-natural-plant-fertilizer-thriving-garden/

Seeds Now. (n.d.). *33 Drought tolerant crops for dry or hot climates.* Www.seedsnow.com. https://www.seedsnow.com/blogs/news/120310727-33-drought-tolerant-crops-for-dry-or-hot-climates

Selemin, J. (2022, November 25). *Benefits of companion planting.* WebMD. https://www.webmd.com/a-to-z-guides/benefits-of-companion-planting

Seven in 10 Americans Say Gardening Allows Them to Gain Control over What They Eat. Digitalhub US. Last modified October 4, 2021. https://swnsdigital.com/us/

2021/08/seven-in-10-americans-say-gardening-has-allowed-them-to-gain-more-control-over-what-they-eat/

Sloan, J. (2023, May 31). *Understanding soil health and biota for farm and garden.* Extension Communications. https://extension.oregonstate.edu/catalog/pub/em-9409-understanding-soil-health-biota-farms-gardens

Strauss, M. (2023, April 12). *Can you grow tomatoes with basil?* Epic Gardening. https://www.epicgardening.com/tomatoes-and-basil/

Swainston, D. (2023, June 1). *12 Drought-tolerant vegetables that will grow well in dry conditions.* Homesandgardens.com. https://www.homesandgardens.com/gardens/best-drought-tolerant-vegetables

Sweetser, R. (2022a, October 25). *Crop rotation 101: Tips for vegetable gardens.* Almanac. https://www.almanac.com/crop-rotation-101-tips-vegetable-gardens

Sweetser, R. (2022b, November 11). *3 Simple DIY soil tests.* Old Farmer's Almanac. https://www.almanac.com/content/3-simple-diy-soil-tests

This Is My Garden. (2022, March 2). *Planting basil with tomato plants - how to grow incredible tomatoes!* https://thisismygarden.com/2022/03/planting-basil-with-tomato-plants/

University of Minnesota Extension. (n.d.). *Growing strawberries in the home garden.* Extension.umn.edu. https://extension.umn.edu/fruit/growing-strawberries-home-garden#harvesting-and-protecting-plants-in-winter--988762

USDA. (n.d.). *Medicinal botany.* https://www.fs.usda.gov/wildflowers/ethnobotany/medicinal/index.shtml#:

Van Elsas, J. D., Chiurazzi, M., Mallon, C. A., Elhottova, D., Kristufek, V., & Salles, J. F. (2012). Microbial diversity determines the invasion of soil by a bacterial pathogen. *Proceedings of the National Academy of Sciences, 109*(4), 1159–1164. https://doi.org/10.1073/pnas.1109326109

Vanderlinden, C. (2023, June 6). *Best (and worst) companion plants for cucumbers.* The Spruce. https://www.thespruce.com/companion-plants-for-cucumbers-2540044

Wikipedia. (2020, November 30). *Companion planting.* https://en.wikipedia.org/wiki/Companion_planting

Xiao, X., Cheng, Z., Meng, H., Liu, L., Li, H., & Dong, Y. (2013). Intercropping of green garlic (allium sativum L.) induces nutrient concentration changes in the soil and plants in continuously cropped cucumber (cucumis sativus L.) in a plastic tunnel. *PLoS ONE, 8*(4), e62173. https://doi.org/10.1371/journal.pone.0062173

Xu, W., Liŭ, D., Wu, F., & Liu, S. (2014). Root exudates of wheat are involved in suppression of Fusarium wilt in watermelon in watermelon-wheat companion cropping. *European Journal of Plant Pathology, 141*(1), 209–216. https://doi.org/10.1007/s10658-014-0528-0

Zhang, M.-M., Wang, N., Hu, Y.-B., & Sun, G.-Y. (2018). Changes in soil physico-chemical properties and soil bacterial community in mulberry (morus alba l.)/alfalfa (medicago sativa L.) intercropping system. *MicrobiologyOpen*, *7*(2), e00555. https://doi.org/10.1002/mbo3.555

Ziton, A. T. (2023, March 27). *Permaculture 101 (definition, examples, pros, cons, & more)*. Couch to Homestead. https://couchtohomestead.com/permaculture-101/#is-permaculture-sustainable.

www.ingramcontent.com/pod-product-compliance
Lightning Source LLC
Chambersburg PA
CBHW071720140626
46557CB00012B/988